NOSH QUICK & EASY

By Joy May

STUDENT — NEW

ISBN: 9780993260988

ISBN: 9780956746405

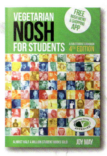

ISBN: 9780993260926

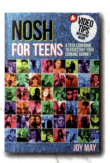

ISBN: 9781838301002

FREE-FROM

ISBN: 9780993260902

ISBN: 9780956746429

ISBN: 9780954317928

ISBN: 9780993260919

FAMILY — ONE — MEAT-FREE

ISBN: 9780956746412

ISBN: 9780993260995

ISBN: 9780956746436

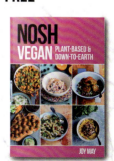

ISBN: 9780993260971

CONTENTS

LETTER FROM JOY...

For some, life is always going to be busy, juggling work, school runs, family, leisure and so on. To help all of us, I have written a book of simple QUICK & EASY recipes, recipes that can be made with the minimum of fuss, many in as little as 20–30 minutes.

Even though the recipes are quick, I have, wherever possible, sought to always use fresh ingredients and avoid processed foods with additives and preservatives.

There are many occasions when we are short of time. I have a section in the book for when we get back home from work, where speed is most important. Also there are quick snacks for the weekend and quick meals for when we have our friends around.

Even though I am cooking every day, trying out new ingredients and combinations, I am always looking for ways to save time and to make things easier. In this book, I pass on tips and ideas that I have picked up along the way that have helped me.

I hope that you will find this book useful and something that takes the hassle out of cooking.

Enjoy.

Joy

P.S. I love to see how people are getting on with my recipes. Why not tweet a photo of your plate using "#noshbooks". I'll be watching out for it!

OUR QUICK & EASY PHILOSOPHY

This book sums up our whole approach to cooking, in that it should be straightforward and down to earth. We found that people loved our approach in "NOSH for Students", our cookbook aimed at university students. In fact, many mums and grans, when buying one for others, told us that they bought one for themselves as well. This got us thinking, what is it about that book that appealed to so many different people? We believe that it is the 'no-fuss' cooking that people like. This is summed up in the way we measure ingredients with a simple mug, rather than weighing scales and measuring jugs.

We have always looked for ways to make recipes clear and easy to follow. Our approach doesn't require lots of kitchen gadgets and doesn't leave your kitchen looking as though you have been visited by a bull in a bad mood! We realise that the cooking process includes the clear up at the end and so we try to keep the pots, pans and utensils to a minimum. In fact, we have rejected recipes for this book purely on how many pans they used.

One of the main challenges of quick cooking has nothing to do with how fast you can dice an onion, or the speed with which you can skip around the kitchen whilst balancing multiple pans on the hob. It's all about quick flavour. Normally, the longer you cook things the more opportunity flavours have to develop. So does quick cooking mean flavourless meals? Certainly not. 'Quick cooking' means we just have to use ingredients that are packed with flavour from the off and using cooking methods that seal in flavour very quickly.

For us, QUICK & EASY means either quick prep and in the oven, or quick prep and on the table, always using easy to follow, hassle-free recipes.

WEAPONS OF CHOICE FOR QUICK & EASY COOKING

I am not going to give you an exhaustive list of every kitchen utensil you might possibly need. Instead, I am just going to suggest a few things that help when trying to cook QUICK & EASY food. I am not one for lots of gadgets in the kitchen; they take up space and end up gathering dust.

2 NON-STICK FRYING PANS

A frying pan is a super-quick way of getting instant heat and flavour into food. There are a number of occasions when, to speed things up, it is good to have two frying pans working alongside each another.

FOOD PROCESSOR

If you have one, USE IT. Keep it on the surface, as it makes big jobs small.

MUG

Simplicity itself. Used for simple measurements where speed is paramount and exactness isn't necessary.

RE-USABLE, SILICON BAKING SHEETS

Stop things sticking during oven-roasting and much quicker to wash up afterwards. I have a few of them, cut to size to fit the baking tins and trays which I use the most. It saves getting out the greaseproof paper and cutting it to size, just for that one meal.

A KNIFE SHARPENER

We always recommend a good, sharp knife, but there is no point having a nice knife if you don't sharpen it. A cheap knife, kept sharp, is better than a brilliant knife, left to go dull.

QUICK & EASY FLAVOURS

In a QUICK & EASY book, we have talked about the need to use ingredients that are packed with instant, fresh flavour. Here are some ideas on achieving this.

FRESHLY GROUND SALT AND BLACK PEPPER

If you have a big tub of table salt in your cooking cupboard, use it for gritting your outside path this winter, or relegate it right away to your cleaning cupboard for soaking up red wine spills on carpets. It is, by no means, the best thing for cooking. Freshly ground sea salt and freshly ground black pepper are a world apart from their pre-ground cousins.

OIL

There are all sorts of oils for all sorts of purposes, but these three oils should get you on your way to great tasting food, fast.

Extra virgin olive oil - we use it in our dressings and it's packed with flavour.

Virgin olive oil - slightly lighter in colour than extra virgin olive oil and is perfect for using in cooking, as it handles higher temperatures better.

Toasted sesame oil - is great in oriental dishes and has a lovely, delicate taste.

HERBS

I have used a lot of fresh herbs in these recipes. Dried herbs are OK in slow cook food as they have time to soak, but in quick cooking, freshness is really important. The cheapest way to get them is to have pots growing on the windowsill in your kitchen. I buy them from the supermarket and, if I remember to water them, they will keep for a few weeks and keep on growing. In the summer, I grow them outside, but using plants from a garden centre which have been accustomed to the outdoors. I have not, as yet, been successful with basil outside; I still keep that herb inside in the summer.

Most frequently used herbs:
basil
coriander
parsley
rosemary

FRESH CHILLIES

Fresh chillies are a great way to get some instant heat in a dish, with a much fresher taste than using a teaspoon of chilli powder. I use the fat, red chillies as the tiny ones tend to be very hot. I always take the seeds out. If you have small children, don't cut the chillies too finely; that way you can just pick them out from the kids' plates. Add chillies towards the end of the cooking time as, the longer they are cooked, the hotter they become.

LEMONS AND LIMES

Lemons and Limes should become part of your staple, weekly shop. They keep well in the fridge and are great to be able to make a salad dressing at a moment's notice, or to freshen-up dishes with a simple squeeze before serving. Both sharp and sweet at the same time, they add heaps of flavour, fast.

HONEY

I love using honey, as you will notice. It is great in dressings, along with lime or lemon, but I also like to use it on fried chicken, fish and meats. It is often added at the last minute, so as not to get burned. Honey is much healthier than processed sugar and gives an immediate, rounded flavour.

TOMATOES

I have used fresh tomatoes in many recipes where you may think it would be easier just to open a tin of chopped tomatoes. However, in many cases, it is really worth the time to chop 6 tomatoes roughly to give a wonderful, fresh taste. Also, there is no need to add the teaspoon of sugar, which can be necessary when using tinned tomatoes.

So, there is my simple list of flavour-boosting ingredients. They are not wildly expensive, but can transform your cooking with ease. Enjoy.

What is quicker than just grabbing a mug and filling it! What is easier to remember as a unit of measure than a mug of this or 2 mugs of that!

Throughout the book, I have used a mug to measure ingredients. This mug holds 1/2 a pint or 300ml of liquid and is the exact size of the mug pictured opposite. So find a mug that measures up to this one and you won't go far wrong.

This book is designed so that you don't need to use any weighing scales or measuring jugs, just our mug and a few spoons. However, for those who like precision, we have included grams and millilitres too.

The mug opposite is the same one I used when writing my first book back in 2000, and it has, therefore, a place in my heart. Although it is now cracked, it still has a special spot in our mug cupboard!

A MUG ≡

ACTUAL SIZE

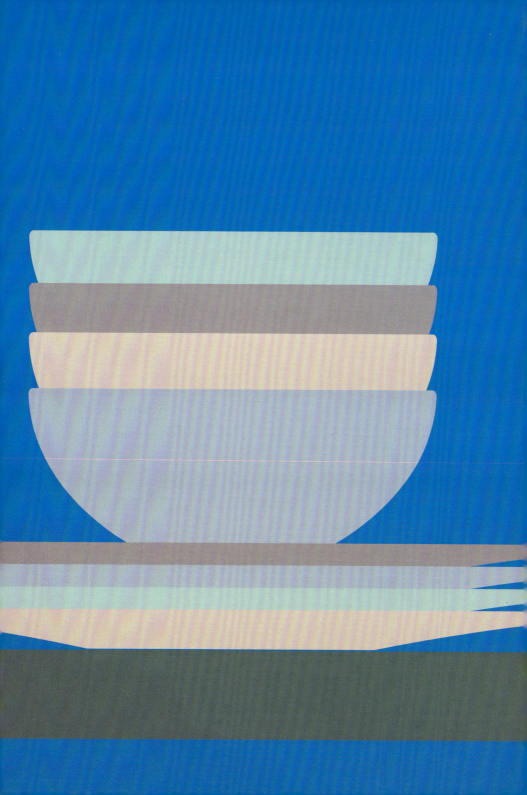

SNACKS

Want a quick snack, but not a sandwich? Here are some great ideas. Ideal for weekend lunches, special breakfasts, or even a quick evening meal. The 'Salmon Tortillas' and 'East End Salad' are two of my favourites.

CAJUN CHICKEN PANNINI

Spicy chicken, gooey cheese and grilled avocado - what more can you say?

2 tablespoons **Cajun seasoning**

2 **chicken breasts**

1 tablespoon **olive oil**

2 small **ciabatta** loaves, cut in half and sliced horizontally

2 tablespoons **mayo**

2 medium **tomatoes**, sliced

1 large **avocado**, peeled and sliced

300g **mozzarella cheese**

1 Put the Cajun seasoning on a plate and press the chicken breasts into it, so that it is evenly distributed.

2 Heat the oil in a frying pan and fry the chicken breasts on a fairly high heat for 2 minutes each side. Turn down the heat and fry for 4 minutes each side, with a lid on the pan. Take care not to burn the Cajun seasoning.

3 Take the chicken out of the pan and leave to rest for a couple of minutes. Slice into thin strips.

4 Toast the ciabatta lightly under the grill. Spread the toasted bread with mayo and arrange the chicken, tomatoes and avocado on the bread.

5 Pull apart the mozzarella and place over the top. Put under the grill for 4–5 minutes, or until the cheese begins to bubble and go brown.

6 Enjoy!

PORK & APPLE BURGERS

If you have leftovers, these burgers are great to eat cold, with the sauce and a little salad.

BURGERS

1 **onion**, grated

1 **Braeburn apple**, grated

500g **minced pork**

1 slice **wholemeal bread**, made into breadcrumbs

1 tablespoon **olive oil**

SAUCE

2 tablespoons **mayo**

1/4 **cucumber**, grated

2 **gherkins**, finely chopped

juice of 1/2 **lemon**

salt and **pepper**

4 **burger buns**

lettuce

1 Squeeze out the excess liquid from the grated onion and apple. Mix together the apple, onion, pork, bread with salt and pepper until the ingredients are evenly distributed. Form 4 burgers.

2 Heat the oil in a frying pan and fry the burgers on a medium heat for about 10 minutes, turning frequently to prevent burning. Check to make sure they are cooked throughout.

3 Meanwhile, mix together the sauce ingredients.

4 Place each one in a bun, together with the lettuce and some of the sauce.

SCAN ME

🌐 **SEE SOME MEDITERRANEAN LAMB BURGERS ONLINE:**
WWW.NOSHBOOKS.COM/LAMB-BURGER

PRAWN & PEA SALAD WITH TARRAGON & MINT

Fresh and delicious and so quick to make. This makes an excellent summer salad.

SALAD

2 mugs (300g) **frozen peas**, defrosted

500g **cooked prawns**

6 **spring onions**, chopped

2 **little gem lettuces**, sliced

2 tablespoons freshly chopped **tarragon**

2 tablespoons freshly chopped **mint**

DRESSING

4 tablespoons **mayo**

juice of a **lemon**

2 tablespoons **extra virgin olive oil**

salt and **pepper**

1 Cook the peas in boiling water for 2 minutes. Drain and rinse under cold water.

2 Mix together the dressing ingredients.

3 Arrange the salad ingredients on 2 plates. Drizzle the dressing over the top.

PAPRIKA SALMON TORTILLAS

Tortillas are an excellent and quick container for many kinds of snack food. The packet of tortillas you buy will probably say to heat them in the microwave. As an alternative, you can brush them lightly with oil and quickly fry them in a frying pan, to wake them up a bit.

GLUTEN-FREE: make sure the tortillas are gluten-free.

DRESSING

4 tablespoons **Greek yogurt**

1/4 **cucumber**, grated

juice of 1/2 **lime**

1 tablespoon **paprika**

salt and **pepper**

4 small **salmon steaks**

1 tablespoon **olive oil**

1 **red cos lettuce**

150g **cherry tomatoes**, halved

handful **fresh coriander**, roughly chopped

4 **corn tortillas**

1 Mix together the dressing ingredients and season.

2 Put the paprika and salt and pepper on a plate and mix. Press the salmon steaks into the mixture. Heat the oil in a frying pan and fry the steaks until the are nicely browned on each side; should take 2–3 minutes each side, depending on the thickness of the steak. Remove from the pan and gently flake.

3 Arrange everything on the tortillas. Serve open or rolled.

ASIAN SPICED BURGERS WITH MANGO SALSA & NAAN 'BUNS'

Try Peshwari naans if you like things a little sweeter. If you have any of the mango salsa left, you can use it with other burgers or cooked meats.

BURGERS

500g **minced beef**

1 **onion**, grated and liquid squeezed out

2 cloves **garlic**, finely chopped

1 tablespoon freshly grated **ginger**

1 tablespoon **garam masala**

salt and **pepper**

2 tablespoons freshly chopped **coriander**

1 tablespoon **olive oil**

MANGO SALSA

1 **mango** peeled and chopped

3 **spring onions**, chopped

1 **fat red chilli**, finely chopped

2 tablespoons freshly chopped **mint**

1 tablespoon freshly chopped **coriander**

zest and juice of a **lime**

1 **Romaine lettuce**

4 small **naan breads**

1 Mix together the burger ingredients in a bowl (apart from the oil). Form into 4 burgers.

2 Heat the oil in a frying pan and add the burgers. Cook on a medium heat for about 10 minutes, turning every now and then. Check one burger to make sure they are cooked through.

3 Meanwhile, mix together the salsa ingredients.

4 Serve the burgers with the lettuce, naans and the salsa.

🎨 GET OUT ALL THE INGREDIENTS BEFORE YOU START; IT MAKES COOKING A LOT CALMER.

SMOKED HADDOCK ROSTI
WITH CRÈME FRAÎCHE DRESSING

Rosti makes a good breakfast or snack meal. The addition of the smoked haddock makes it almost a main meal. It is inexpensive and has a distinctive flavour.

3 medium **potatoes**, grated

300g **smoked haddock**, finely sliced

1 tablespoon **olive**

DRESSING

4 tablespoons **crème fraîche**

juice of a **lemon**

1 tablespoon freshly chopped **parsley** or **basil**

1 bag **rocket salad**

1 Squeeze the moisture out of the potatoes. Place in a bowl with the haddock and season well. Mix together and divide into eight lots.

2 Heat the oil in a large frying pan. Place 4 lots of the mixture at a time in the pan and press down to flatten. Fry on a medium heat for 6–8 minutes until browned on both sides and cooked through.

3 Mix the dressing ingredients in a bowl, season with salt and pepper, and serve everything together.

CORN CAKES WITH AVOCADO SALAD

DRESSING

juice of a **lime**
2 tablespoons **extra virgin olive oil**
salt and **pepper**
1 teaspoon **granulated sugar**

CORN CAKES

2 **eggs**
3/4 mug (150g) **self-raising flour**
1 tablespoon **crème fraîche**
325g tin **sweetcorn**, drained
1 bunch **spring onions**, chopped
1 tablespoon freshly chopped **basil**
1 tablespoon freshly chopped **chives**

2 tablespoons **olive oil**
4 slices bread or a small
ciabatta loaf, sliced

SALAD

1 **avocado**, cut into small chunks
1 bag **salad leaves**
4 medium **tomatoes**
2 tablespoons **extra virgin olive oil**

1 Mix the dressing ingredients together.

2 Beat together the eggs and flour. Add the crème fraîche and the drained sweetcorn, spring onions and herbs and mix well. Season with salt and pepper.

3 Heat the 2 tablespoons of oil in a large frying pan. Add the bread and fry on both sides until browned. Cut into strips or croutons.

4 Add the corn mixture to the frying pan, 1 tablespoon at a time, and cook on a medium heat until browned on both sides and cooked through.

5 Mix the salad ingredients together and serve the corn cakes on top. Drizzle the dressing over the salad.

SCAN ME

🌐 WE HAVE A 'COURGETTE FRITTERS' RECIPE ONLINE:
WWW.NOSHBOOKS.COM/FRITTERS

PASTRAMI ON RYE SALAD

This is a take on the American 'Pastrami on Rye', but made into a gorgeous salad. If you are not keen on the gherkins, then you can replace them with normal cucumber.

GLUTEN-FREE: use a good, nutty GF bread, instead of the rye.

CROUTONS

1 tablespoon **olive oil**

3 slices **rye bread**

DRESSING

3 tablespoons **extra virgin olive oil**

juice of a **lime**

1/2 teaspoon **granulated sugar**

salt and **pepper**

SALAD

250g **cherry tomatoes**, halved

6 **gherkins**, sliced

4 **celery sticks**, sliced

1 tablespoon freshly chopped **basil**

1 tablespoon freshly chopped **parsley**

6 **spring onions**, chopped

1 bag **salad leaves**

6 **spring onions**

120g **pastrami**

1 Heat 1 tablespoon oil in a large frying pan and add the slices of rye bread. Fry until browned on both sides. Take out of the pan and cut into croutons.

2 Mix the dressing ingredients together in a bowl.

3 Mix the salad ingredients and croutons together in a large bowl. Divide the mixture between 4 plates. Sprinkle over the dressing.

4 Arrange the pastrami on top and serve.

TUNA NIÇOISE

A 'Tuna Niçoise' would normally have new potatoes in it, but we thought we would mess with the old classic and see how it went. We liked it, so here it is.

GLUTEN-FREE: use GF pasta.

---

4 **eggs**

2 mugs (200g) **pasta** (we used Fusilli)

200g **green beans**

DRESSING

juice of a **lemon**

4 tablespoons **mayo**

2 tablespoons **extra virgin olive oil**

salt and **pepper**

1 teaspoon **granulated sugar**

SALAD

2 x 185g tins **tuna**

30 **olives**

12 **anchovies**

6 **spring onions**, chopped

250g **cherry tomatoes**, halved

1 tablespoon freshly chopped **basil**

1 Boil the eggs for 7 minutes and run under cold water until the eggs are cool enough to handle. Gently peel and set to one side until needed.

2 Cook the pasta in a pan of salted, boiling water. Add the green beans for the final 5 minutes of cooking. Drain, rinse under the cold tap and return to the pan.

3 Mix together the dressing ingredients.

4 Arrange the salad between the 4 plates and drizzle over the dressing.

NEVER WAIT FOR WATER TO BOIL IN A PAN. BOIL THE WATER IN THE KETTLE FIRST.

TROUT ON CIABATTA WITH CORIANDER YOGURT DRESSING

This posh 'on toast' snack is so delicious and is great if you have a few folk around for a quick lunch.

DRESSING

6 tablespoons **Greek yogurt**

4 **spring onions**, finely chopped

6 **anchovy fillets**, chopped

3 tablespoons freshly chopped **coriander**

salt and **pepper**

4 **eggs**

1 tablespoon **olive oil**

400g **trout fillets**

8 thick slices **ciabatta** or **crusty bread**

1 clove **garlic**

1　Mix together the dressing ingredients and set to one side until needed.

2　Put the eggs in a pan of boiling water and bring to the boil, simmering for 7 minutes. Drain the boiling water away, fill the pan with cold water and leave for 2 minutes. Peel the eggs, but be careful as they will still be soft.

3　Heat the oil in a frying pan and fry the trout for about 2 minutes each side, depending on the thickness. The trout will be cooked quite quickly. Transfer to a plate, remove any skin and flake the flesh off the skin.

4　Toast the ciabatta, cut the garlic clove in half and rub the garlic over the toast.

5　Serve the dressing and the trout on the ciabatta. Season with salt and pepper.

EAST END SALAD

We called this 'East End Salad' because it is a bit like ham, egg and chips, but the spinach gives it a healthier twist.

1 tablespoon **olive oil**

4 medium **potatoes**, cut into chunks

200g pack **streaky bacon**

4 **eggs**

200g pack **baby spinach leaves**

6 **spring onions**, chopped

DRESSING

1 teaspoon **mustard**

1 tablespoon **runny honey**

2 tablespoons **extra virgin olive oil**

juice of a **lemon**

1 Heat the oil in a large frying pan. Add the potatoes and season well with salt and pepper. Keep on a medium heat, with a lid on the pan, and fry for about 15 minutes. Keep turning the potatoes to allow them to brown on all sides.

2 Meanwhile, fry the bacon until crisp. Drain on some kitchen paper. Cut into bite-size pieces.

3 Put the eggs in boiling water and simmer for 6 minutes. Run under cold water and peel.

4 Mix together the spinach and onions.

5 Mix together the dressing ingredients and season. Add the spinach mixture and mix well.

6 Arrange the spinach, bacon, potatoes and eggs on plates.

⏱ NEVER WAIT FOR WATER TO BOIL IN A PAN. BOIL THE WATER IN THE KETTLE FIRST.

PANZANELLA SALAD WITH OLIVES & CAPERS

GLUTEN-FREE: use GF bread.

DRESSING

3 tablespoons **extra virgin olive oil**

1 tablespoon freshly chopped **basil**

2 tablespoons **red wine vinegar**

1 teaspoon **granulated sugar**

salt and **pepper**

SALAD

2 **ready-roasted red peppers**, sliced

250g **cherry tomatoes**
or 6 medium **tomatoes**, cut into chunks

6 **spring onions**, sliced

20 **green olives**, halved

2 tablespoons **capers**

1 **fat red chilli**, chopped

1 bag **salad leaves**

CROUTONS

2 tablespoons **olive oil**

4 slices **wholemeal bread**

1   Mix together the dressing ingredients in a large bowl.

2   Add the salad ingredients and toss together. Divide between the four plates.

3   Heat the oil in a large frying pan. Add the bread and fry, on each side, until browned. Cut into croutons, sprinkle over the salad and serve.

HONEY & SOY NOODLES

This little noodle salad is packed with flavour. The sweetness of the honey and the richness of the egg are just wonderful together.

GLUTEN-FREE: use GF soy sauce and use rice noodles.

4 nests **dried egg noodles**

200g **green beans**, cut in half

1 small **broccoli**, cut into thin strips

2 tablespoons **toasted sesame oil**

6 **spring onions**, chopped

4 medium **tomatoes**, chopped

1 tablespoon freshly grated **ginger**

2 tablespoons **soy sauce**

2 tablespoons **runny honey**

4 **eggs**

1 Put the noodles, broccoli and green beans in a pan of boiling water and simmer for 5 minutes. Once cooked, drain and set to one side until needed.

2 Meanwhile, heat 1 tablespoon of the sesame oil in a wok and fry the spring onions, tomatoes and ginger for 2 minutes. Add the soy and honey and heat through. Add the noodle mixture and mix well.

3 Put the other tablespoon of sesame oil into a frying pan and fry the 4 eggs until crispy round the edges. Serve them on top of the noodle mixture.

ROAST MUSHROOMS STUFFED WITH GOATS' CHEESE

GLUTEN-FREE: use GF bread.

8 **portobello mushrooms**

3 tablespoons **olive oil**

1 tablespoon **balsamic vinegar**

4 medium **tomatoes**, sliced

2 x 120g packets **goats' cheese**

2 slices **bread**, made into breadcrumbs

1 tablespoon **olive oil**

1 bag **mixed salad**

1 Preheat the oven to 180°C fan/200°C/gas 6.

2 Take the stalks out of the mushrooms. Lightly grease a roasting tray and place the mushrooms, bottom side up, on the tray. Mix together the oil and balsamic vinegar and drizzle over the mushrooms. Season well and place in the oven for 10 minutes.

3 Take the tray out of the oven and place the sliced tomatoes and goats' cheese on top of each mushroom. Mix the breadcrumbs and the oil together and sprinkle over the mushrooms. Return to the oven for a further 10 minutes. The breadcrumbs should be lightly browned and the cheese beginning to melt.

4 Serve with the salad leaves.

IF YOU HAVE A FOOD PROCESSOR, USE IT! DON'T KEEP IT IN A CUPBOARD, BUT HAVE IT ON A WORK SURFACE, HOWEVER SMALL YOUR KITCHEN IS. IT SAVES LOADS OF TIME AND ENERGY.

SPINACH & GOATS CHEESE FRITTATA

6 **eggs**

1/2 teaspoon freshly grated **nutmeg** (optional)

2 tablespoons **water**

1 tablespoon **olive oil**

1 medium **leek**, chopped

4 **spring onions**, chopped

1 **roasted red pepper** (from a jar), roughly chopped

100g pack **baby spinach**

2 medium **tomatoes**, sliced

125g pack **soft goats' cheese**, sliced

1 bag **green salad**

1 Preheat the grill.

2 Beat the eggs, nutmeg and water together and season with salt and pepper.

3 Heat the oil in a frying pan and add the leeks and onions. Fry until the leeks just begin to soften.

4 Add the peppers and spinach and fry until the spinach begins to wilt.

5 Add the egg mixture. Fry until the egg begins to set and then gently move the set egg, so that the unset egg can reach the bottom of the pan.

6 When most of the egg is set, take off the heat and add the tomatoes and goats' cheese. Place under the grill until the frittata begins to brown and rises a little.

7 Serve with salad.

SCAN ME

🌐 **WE LOVE FRITTATAS. HERE'S ANOTHER ONE:**
WWW.NOSHBOOKS.COM/SWEET-POTATO

MINESTRONE SOUP

2 tablespoons **olive oil**

150g **pancetta lardons**

1 **onion**, thinly sliced

1 **carrot**, peeled and cut into small chunks

2 sticks **celery**, finely sliced

1 clove **garlic**, finely chopped

400g tin **butter beans**, drained and rinsed

3 mugs (900ml) **water**

2 tablespoons **tomato purée**

1 **chicken stock cube**

½ mug (50g) **macaroni**

100g **spinach**, roughly chopped

¼ mug (15g) grated **Parmesan**

1 Heat the oil in a large saucepan and add the pancetta, onion, carrot, celery and garlic. Fry for 5 minutes, stirring frequently.

2 Add the beans, water, tomato purée, stock and macaroni. Simmer for another 5 minutes.

3 Add the spinach (you don't need to cook as it will wilt immediately in the soup).

4 Serve with the grated Parmesan over the top.

GET OUT ALL THE INGREDIENTS BEFORE YOU START; IT MAKES COOKING A LOT CALMER.

CHORIZO ROSTI WITH SPINACH & POACHED EGGS

Rosti is quite versatile. Here, we have added some chorizo, and the flavour permeates through the potatoes. I love the egg and spinach combination. Altogether, a great meal. If you are not sure about poaching eggs, visit our website www.noshbooks.com.

GLUTEN-FREE: make sure the chorizo is gluten-free.

4 medium **potatoes**, grated
200g **diced chorizo**
1 tablespoon **olive oil**
4 **eggs**
200g **spinach**

1 Squeeze the excess moisture from the grated potatoes and mix with the chorizo. Season well with salt and pepper.

2 Make 4 rosti out of the mixture. Heat the oil in a large frying pan and place the rosti in the pan. Fry on a medium heat until the potatoes are browned and cooked through. Usually takes about 10 minutes.

3 Meanwhile, poach the eggs in a frying pan half-filled with gently simmering water.

4 Once the rostis are cooked, take them out of the pan and drain on some kitchen paper. Add the spinach to the hot pan; it will wilt in about 1 minute.

5 Serve the spinach on top of the hash brown, with the egg on top.

SCAN ME

🌐 **WE DID A VIDEO ON HOW TO POACH EGGS, CHECK IT OUT HERE:**
WWW.NOSHBOOKS.COM/POACHING-EGGS

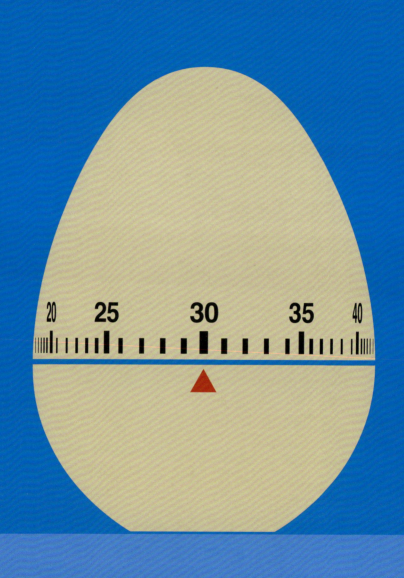

30 MINUTES OR QUICKER

Running short on time, but still want something special to eat? All of these meals are designed with speed in mind and should be on the table in a flash.

PRAWN & CHORIZO PASTA

You can buy frozen prawns if you like, they are significantly cheaper and work just as well as fresh prawns in dishes like this.

GLUTEN-FREE: use rice instead of pasta and a GF stock cubes and chorizo.

1 1/2 mugs (375g) **orzo** or **trofie pasta**

1 **chicken stock cube**

1 teaspoon **ground turmeric**

1 tablespoon **olive oil**

1 **red pepper**, chopped

200g **chorizo sausage**, diced

300g **cooked prawns**

6 **spring onions**, chopped

1 mug (150g) **frozen peas**, defrosted

2 tablespoons freshly chopped **basil**

juice of a **lemon**

1 Cook the pasta in a pan of boiling, water. Add the stock cube and turmeric and mix well. Simmer for 4–5 minutes, or until the pasta is just cooked. Drain the pasta and return to the pan.

2 Heat the oil in a wok, add the peppers and fry until they begin to soften. Add the chorizo and fry until it begins to brown.

3 Add the prawns, spring onions peas, basil and pasta to the pan and heat through.

4 Squeeze over the lemon juice and season well with salt and pepper.

BALSAMIC CHICKEN WITH CREAMY MASH

This balsamic sauce is rich and sooo yummy. Ben and Tim dipped all the spare bits of everything in it as the photograph was taken, a sure sign that it tasted good.

GLUTEN-FREE: make sure the stock cubes are gluten-free.

MASH

5 medium **potatoes**, peeled and cut into chunks

25g **butter**, measure using packet

2 tablespoons **double cream**

BALSAMIC SAUCE

25g **butter**, measure using packet

1 tablespoon **olive oil**

2 **red onions**, sliced

1 sprig **rosemary leaves**, chopped

6 tablespoons **balsamic vinegar**

2 tablespoons **runny honey**

1/2 mug (150ml) **water**

1 **chicken stock cube**

1 tablespoon **olive oil**

4 **chicken breasts**

sprouting broccoli

1 Put the potatoes in boiling water, bring to the boil and then turn down to simmer for 10 minutes. Drain, return to the pan and mash with the 25g butter and cream. Season well.

2 Meanwhile, heat the butter and 1 tablespoon of oil in a saucepan and fry the onions until they begin to brown. Add the rosemary, balsamic, honey, water and stock cube. Season well, bring to the boil and then simmer for 10 minutes.

3 Heat 1 tablespoon of olive oil in a small frying pan and add the chicken breasts. Cook on a fairly high heat for 2 minutes each side. Turn down the heat to medium and fry for 4 minutes each side, with a lid on the pan. Cook for less time if the chicken breasts are small.

4 Put the sprouting broccoli in boiling water and then turn down to simmer for 4–5 minutes.

5 Serve everything together.

PENNE BOSCAIOLA

'Boscaiola' is Italian for 'woodcutter' or 'lumberjack'. He would typically gather mushrooms from the woods. This is a classic Italian dish which contains mushrooms, bacon and a creamy pasta.

GLUTEN-FREE: use GF pasta.

3 mugs (300g) **penne pasta**

1 tablespoon **olive oil**

200g **streaky bacon**, sliced

6 **spring onions**, chopped

250g **chestnut mushrooms**, sliced

300ml **single cream**

1/2 mug (30g) grated **Parmesan**

1 tablespoon freshly chopped **basil**

1 Cook the pasta in a pan of salted, boiling water. Drain and return to the pan until needed.

2 Heat the oil in a large saucepan or wok. Fry the bacon until it begins to brown.

3 Add the onions and the mushrooms and fry for 2–3 minutes.

4 Add the cream and Parmesan and season to taste. Bring to the boil.

5 Add the pasta and the chopped basil and serve immediately.

SCAN ME

🌐 **FOR A PASTITSIO RECIPE, GO TO:**
WWW.NOSHBOOKS.COM/PASTITSIO

PASTA AMATRICIANA

Amatriciana is a classic Italian dish. It usually has bacon, tomato and basil, but here we have replaced the bacon with pancetta, which makes it a bit simpler to make.

GLUTEN-FREE: use GF pasta and stock cube.

2 mugs **pasta** (200g) (we used Fusilli)

2 tablespoons **olive oil**

1 **onion**, chopped

2 cloves **garlic**, finely chopped

200g **pancetta lardons**

6 medium **tomatoes**, roughly chopped

1/2 **fat red chilli**, finely chopped

2 tablespoons **tomato purée**

1/2 mug (150ml) **water**

1 **vegetable stock cube**

2 tablespoons freshly chopped **basil**

1 mug (60g) grated **Parmesan**

1 Cook the pasta in a pan of salted, boiling water. Once cooked, drain and return to the pan.

2 Meanwhile, heat the oil in a wok or large frying pan and add the onion and garlic. Fry until they begin to soften.

3 Add the pancetta lardons to the pan and fry until they begin to brown.

4 Add the tomatoes, chilli, tomato purée, water and stock and bring to the boil. Turn down to simmer for 5 minutes.

5 Add the pasta, basil and Parmesan and mix.

6 Serve immediately.

NEVER WAIT FOR WATER TO BOIL IN A PAN. BOIL THE WATER IN THE KETTLE FIRST.

CHORIZO & CHILLI RIGATONI

Chorizo has a hearty flavour which infuses pasta dishes well. I buy packets of chopped chorizo which will keep in the fridge for a week or two. This is always very handy.

GLUTEN-FREE: make sure the chorizo and pasta are gluten-free.

2 ½ mugs (250g) **Rigatoni**

1 tablespoon **olive oil**

200g **chorizo**, sliced

1 **fat red chilli**, deseeded and finely chopped

2 sprigs **rosemary**, chopped

6 medium **tomatoes**, chopped into chunks

1 tablespoon **tomato purée**

4 tablespoons **crème fraîche**

½ teaspoon **granulated sugar**

1 Put the pasta on to cook in a large saucepan. Once cooked, drain and return to the pan with a lid on.

2 Meanwhile, heat the oil in a large frying pan, or wok, and fry the chorizo for 2 minutes. Drain the excess oil from the pan.

3 Add the chilli and rosemary to the frying pan. Fry for 1 minute, being careful not to let things burn. Add the rest of the ingredients, season and stir together.

4 Add the pasta to the pan.

OLIVE & TUNA PASTA

Tuna can be a really handy staple to make less expensive dishes. Be careful not to stir it too much after the tuna is added, otherwise it will be a bit mushy.

GLUTEN-FREE: use GF pasta and stock cubes.

2 mugs (200g) **pasta** (we used Ditaloni)

1 tablespoon **olive oil**

6 **spring onions**, chopped

1 clove **garlic**, finely chopped

6 large **tomatoes**, chopped

2 tablespoons **tomato purée**

¼ mug (75ml) **water**

1 **veg stock cube**

10 **black olives** , roughly chopped

10 **green olives**, roughly chopped

2 tablespoons freshly chopped **basil**

6 **anchovy fillets**, roughly chopped

2 x 185g tins **tuna**, drained

1 Cook the pasta in a pan of salted, boiling water. Drain and return to the pan.

2 Meanwhile, heat the oil in a wok or large frying pan. Fry the onions, garlic and tomatoes until they begin to soften.

3 Add the tomato purée, water and stock cube. Season well and simmer for 2 minutes.

4 Add the olives, basil, anchovies and flaked tuna, along with the cooked pasta, and mix.

TARRAGON & CHICKEN RIGATONI

Tarragon can grow well outdoors, either in a pot or planted in the ground, and will keep going throughout the winter. It has a lovely aniseed/vanilla flavour, which makes this a delicious and slightly unusual dish.

GLUTEN-FREE: use GF pasta and stock cube.

2 ½ mugs (250g) **rigatoni**

50g **butter**, measure using packet

2 large **leeks**, sliced

2 cloves **garlic**, chopped

3 **chicken breasts**, cut into chunks

250g **chestnut mushrooms**, sliced

300ml **single cream**

1 **chicken stock cube**

2 tablespoons freshly chopped **tarragon**, or 1 teaspoon **dried tarragon**

1 Put the pasta in a pan of boiling water. Bring to the boil and then turn down to simmer for 7–8 minutes, or until the pasta is just cooked. Don't overcook. Drain and set to one side.

2 Heat the butter in a wok or large frying pan and add the leeks and the garlic. Fry on a medium heat for 3–4 minutes until the leeks begin to soften.

3 Add the chicken to the pan and cook for 3–4 minutes, until the chicken begins to brown on the outside and is no longer pink.

4 Add the mushrooms and fry for 1 minute. Add the cream, stock cube and tarragon, bring to the boil and simmer for 2 minutes. Season with salt and pepper.

5 Add the pasta to the chicken mixture.

 £ 1.61 /PERSON SERVES 4 EASE ★★☆☆☆ PREP 20 MINS GF OPTION

CHICKEN CHILLI TORTILLA PIE

Obviously, if you like things really spicy you can add another chilli and use spicy tortillas. Kids will love this one. We have made it in individual dishes, but it works just as well in one big one.

GLUTEN-FREE: make sure the tortillas and stock cube are gluten-free.

1 tablespoon **olive oil**

1 **onion**, sliced

1 clove **garlic**, finely chopped

3 **chicken breasts**, cut into chunks

125g **mushrooms**, sliced

6 medium **tomatoes**, chopped

1/2 mug (150ml) **water**

1 **chicken stock cube**

2 tablespoons **tomato purée**

1 **fat red chilli**, deseeded and chopped

175g bag **tortilla chips**

1 mug (75g) grated **Cheddar cheese**

1   Preheat the grill.

2   Heat the oil in a large frying pan or wok. Add the onion and garlic and fry until the onion begins to soften.

3   Add the chicken and fry until no longer pink.

4   Add the mushrooms and fry for 1 minute.

5   Add the tomatoes, water, stock cube, tomato purée and chilli. Bring to the boil and simmer for 5 minutes. Season with salt and pepper.

6   Pour into a casserole dish. Pile the tortilla chips on top and then the grated cheese.

7   Place under the grill for about 2 minutes. The cheese should be melted and the chips beginning to brown.

SCAN ME

🌐 **WE MADE ANOTHER TORTILLA PIE HERE:**
WWW.NOSHBOOKS.COM/TORTILLA-PIE

SPANISH PRAWN RISOTTO

GLUTEN-FREE: make sure the chorizo and stock cube are gluten-free.

2 tablespoons **olive oil**

1 **red pepper**, cut into small chunks

200g **chorizo**, cut into small chunks

2 cloves **garlic**, finely chopped

6 medium **tomatoes**, chopped

6 **spring onions**, sliced

1 mug (215g) **risotto rice**

2 mugs (600ml) **water**

1 **vegetable stock cube**

400g **raw prawns**, defrost if frozen

1   Heat the oil in a frying pan. Add the peppers and chorizo and fry until the chorizo begins to brown.

2   Add the garlic, tomatoes and onions and fry for 30 seconds.

3   Add the rice and fry until it absorbs the juices from the pan.

4   Add the water and stock and bring to the boil. Turn down to simmer, with a lid on the pan, for 15 minutes, or until the rice is tender.

5   Add the prawns and cook until they turn pink. Take off the heat and season with salt and pepper.

LAMB KHEEMA WITH NAAN BREAD

You may have heard of Kheema before in Indian restaurants, where it is a type of naan bread. Don't worry, we are not going to ask you to make naan breads! Kheema is basically a traditional Indian dish that contains lamb mince.

GLUTEN-FREE: use GF stock cubes and serve with rice, instead of naans if you can't find GF naans.

1 tablespoon **olive oil**

1 **onion**, sliced

1 tablespoon freshly grated **ginger**

1 tablespoon **fennel seeds**

1 teaspoon **cumin seeds**

1 teaspoon **ground tumeric**

500g **minced lamb**

2 small **sweet potatoes**, peeled and cut into chunks

2 medium **tomatoes**, chopped

1 mug (300ml) **water**

1 **lamb stock cube**

3 **bay leaves**

1 mug (150g) **frozen peas**, defrosted

1 **fat red chilli**, chopped

1 tablespoon freshly chopped **mint**

naan breads

1 Heat the oil in a wok or large saucepan. Add the onion and spices and fry for 1 minute.

2 Add the mince and fry until it is no longer pink.

3 Add the sweet potatoes, tomatoes, water, stock and bay leaves. Bring to the boil and then turn down and simmer for 20 minutes. Stir occasionally.

4 Add the peas, chilli and mint and heat through.

5 Serve with naan breads.

GET OUT ALL THE INGREDIENTS BEFORE YOU START; IT MAKES COOKING A LOT CALMER.

SAFFRON CHICKEN & NUT PILAF

If you do not have any saffron, just use a teaspoon of pilau rice seasoning. Delicious, mild and delicate flavour come from the nuts and saffron and little pops of sweetness come from the raisins.

1 pinch **saffron** or 1 teaspoon **pilau rice seasoning**

25g **butter**, measure using packet

2 **onions**, chopped

3 **chicken breasts**, cut into small chunks

1 **cinnamon stick**

1 tablespoon freshly grated **ginger**

4 tablespoons **raisins**

1 ½ mugs (375g) **basmati rice**

2 tablespoons **pine nuts**

2 tablespoons **cashew nuts**

1 Put the saffron (or pilau rice seasoning) in a mug of boiling water and allow to infuse.

2 Heat the butter in a wok, or large frying pan, and add the onions. Fry until they begin to soften.

3 Add the chicken and fry for 1–2 minutes until it is no longer pink. Add the mug of saffron water.

4 Add the cinnamon stick, ginger, raisins, rice and 2 more mugs of boiling water. Season well.

5 Bring everything to the boil, mixing well. Turn down to simmer for 10 minutes, with a lid or foil over the pan.

6 Sprinkle over the nuts and stir in. Put the pan on a high heat, with the lid off, and allow the mixture to get dry. Allow the bottom of the mixture to brown a little. Stir in the brown crunchy bits and then allow the next 'bottom layer' to brown. Stir again.

7 Take out the cinnamon stick and serve immediately.

SPEEDY PORK BOLOGNESE

The prep for this is so quick - just pop everything in and let the food processor do all the work. If you don't have a food processor, just chop everything finely. If you don't have sun-dried tomato purée, just use regular tomato purée.

GLUTEN-FREE: use GF pasta and stock cubes.

1 **onion**

2 sticks **celery**

1 **carrot**

1 **red apple**, cored

1 clove **garlic**

2 tablespoons **olive oil**

500g **minced pork**

500g **passata**

1 **vegetable stock cube**

1 tablespoon **sun-dried tomato purée**

400g **spaghetti**

2 tablespoons freshly chopped **parsley**

Parmesan to serve

1 Put the onion, celery, carrot, apple and garlic in a food processor and blitz until it is evenly chopped.

2 Heat the oil in a wok or large saucepan. Add the veggies and cook on a fairly high heat for 5 minutes. Keep stirring.

3 Add the mince and cook until it is no longer pink.

4 Add the passata, veg stock cube and tomato purée. Season well and simmer for 10 minutes.

5 Meanwhile, cook the pasta in a pan of salted, boiling water. Drain and leave to one side until needed.

6 Add the parsley to the bolognese and heat through for 30 seconds.

7 Mix the pasta and sauce together. Grate the Parmesan on top to serve.

> 📷 IF YOU HAVE A FOOD PROCESSOR, USE IT! DON'T KEEP IT IN A CUPBOARD, BUT HAVE IT ON A WORK SURFACE, HOWEVER SMALL YOUR KITCHEN IS. IT SAVES LOADS OF TIME AND ENERGY.

PRAWN & SPINACH RISOTTO

Delightfully light, but tasty dish. Really quick and simple to make. The spinach is hardly cooked at all, so keeps all its glorious goodness.

GLUTEN-FREE: use GF stock cubes.

2 tablespoons **olive oil**

1 **onion**, finely chopped

1 mug (215g) **risotto rice**

2 mugs (600ml) **water**

2 **fish stock cubes**

450g **king prawns**, defrosted

200g **spinach**, roughly chopped

½ mug (30g) grated **Parmesan**

juice of a **lemon**

1 Heat the oil in a wok, add the onions and fry until they begin to soften.

2 Add the rice and fry for 1 minute, to allow the rice to absorb the juices in the pan.

3 Add the water and the stock, bring to the boil and then turn down to simmer, with a lid on the pan, for 10–12 minutes, or until the rice is tender. Stir the risotto occasionally and add more water if necessary. Risotto should not be dry, but have a creamy consistency.

4 Once the rice is tender, add the prawns and spinach and heat through for 3–4 minutes, with the lid on the pan.

5 Stir in the Parmesan and lemon juice. Season well with salt and pepper. Serve hot.

SCAN ME

🌐 **FANCY A SPICY RISOTTO? GO TO:**
WWW.NOSHBOOKS.COM/RISOTTO

CIDER SAUSAGES WITH LEEK & POTATO MASH

Excellent way of dressing up 'bangers and mash' and making it a bit more special. Use a sharp knife to cut the sausage skins, lengthways, down one side, and you will be able to easily peel them.

GLUTEN-FREE: make sure the sausages and flour are gluten-free.

5 medium **potatoes**, peeled and cut into chunks

50g **butter**, measure using packet

3 **leeks**, sliced

1 tablespoon **olive oil**

8 **sausages**, skinned and each pinched into 4 pieces

1 **onion**, sliced

2 tablespoons **plain flour**

2 mugs (600ml) **cider**

1 Simmer the potatoes, in a pan of salted, boiling water, for 10 minutes. Drain and return to the pan. Add 25g of butter, mash and put a lid on to keep warm.

2 Meanwhile, heat the remaining butter in a large frying pan and fry the leeks until they begin to brown. Add to the mashed potato and mix together. Set to one side, with the lid on, until needed.

3 Using the same frying pan, heat 1 tablespoon of oil and fry the sausages and onion until they are browned.

4 Add the flour to the frying pan and mix. Add the cider, stir and then simmer for 2–3 minutes. The sauce should thicken.

5 Season well with salt and pepper. Serve with the mash.

MACKEREL IN CURRIED COUSCOUS SALAD

Smoked mackerel has a strong, distinctive flavour. You can buy it vacuum packed and cooked, so no need to have a strong fish smell in the kitchen. Unopened, it will keep in the fridge for ages, so very handy.

1 tablespoon **Rogan Josh curry paste**

2 mugs (600ml) **boiling water**

1 mug (200g) **couscous**

1/2 mug (90g) **sultanas**

250g **smoked mackerel fillets**, skinned and flaked

4 **spring onions**, chopped

1/2 **red pepper**, chopped

2 medium **tomatoes**, chopped

1 tablespoon freshly chopped **coriander**

1/2 **cucumber**, diced

juice of a **lemon**

1 Put the curry paste in a bowl, add the boiling water and stir. Add the couscous and sultanas and cover. Leave for 5 minutes.

2 Add the rest of the ingredients and gently stir. Season with salt and pepper.

CORONATION CHICKEN SALAD

This is a take on the old fashioned 'Coronation Chicken'. It has a lovely delicate taste. The mango in the salad provides a freshness to the whole dish.

GLUTEN-FREE: make sure the curry paste is gluten-free.

MANGO RICE SALAD

3/4 mug (190g) **basmati rice**

1 **mango**, peeled and cut into small chunks

2 tablespoons freshly chopped **coriander**

6 **spring onions**, chopped

1 **green apple**, chopped into small pieces

2 tablespoons **toasted flaked almonds**

1 tablespoon **Korma curry paste**

juice of a **lemon**

3 **chicken breasts**, cut into chunks

1 tablespoon **olive oil**

SAUCE

3 tablespoons **mayo**

1 tablespoon **mango chutney**

1 tablespoon **Greek yogurt**

salt and **pepper**

2 tablespoons freshly chopped **coriander**

1 Put the rice in 1 1/2 mugs boiling water. Simmer, with a lid on the pan, for 10 minutes. Take out of the pan to cool a little.

2 Mix together the rest of the mango rice salad ingredients in a bowl, season, and add the rice when it has cooled slightly.

3 Mix the curry paste, lemon juice and chicken. Heat the oil in a frying pan and fry the chicken pieces on a medium heat, until they are cooked through and nicely browned.

4 Mix together the sauce ingredients.

5 Arrange the rice and the chicken on the plates, sprinkle over the coriander and drizzle over the sauce.

CHICKEN, BACON & AVOCADO SALAD

1 tablespoon **olive oil**

8 slices **bacon**

3 **chicken breasts**

2 teaspoons **runny honey**

2 tablespoons **sesame seeds**

DRESSING

2 tablespoons **extra virgin olive oil**

juice of a **lime**

1 teaspoon **runny honey**

salt and **pepper**

1 bag **salad leaves**

250g **cherry tomatoes**, halved

1/2 **cucumber**, cut into sticks

1 **avocado**, peeled and sliced

1   Heat the oil in a frying pan and add the bacon. Cook until crispy. Remove from the pan and cut into small pieces. The bacon will almost crumble.

2   Add the chicken breasts to the pan. Season with salt and pepper. Fry for 2 minutes, each side, on a fairly high heat.

3   Turn down the heat and fry, with a lid on the pan, for 4 minutes on each side.

4   Turn over the chicken breasts, pour the honey over them, and sprinkle with the sesame seeds. Fry for 1 minute each side, being careful not to burn the honey. Remove from the pan and cut into slices.

5   Mix the dressing ingredients together.

6   Arrange the salad leaves, tomatoes, cucumber and avocado on the plates. Put the chicken over the top, then the bacon, and finally drizzle with the dressing.

SWEET POTATO, BACON & ORZO PASTA SALAD

2 large **sweet potatoes**, peeled and cut into chunks

2 tablespoons **olive oil**

1 mug (250g) **orzo pasta**

2 mugs (300g) **frozen peas**, defrosted

200g **streaky bacon**

6 **spring onions**, chopped

1 tablespoon freshly chopped **mint**

100g **feta cheese**

1 Preheat the oven to 200°C fan/220°C/gas 7.

2 Mix the sweet potatoes with the 2 tablespoons olive oil, season with salt and pepper, and place on a large baking tray. Put in the oven for 25 minutes, or until the potatoes are tender and lightly browned.

3 Meanwhile, put the pasta in salted, boiling water and simmer for 3 minutes. Add the peas to the pan for the last 2 minutes of cooking. Drain and return to the pan.

4 Fry or grill the bacon until it is browned and crispy. Cut into bite-sized pieces.

5 Mix everything together, apart from the feta. Divide between the plates and crumble the feta over the top. Season with salt and pepper.

£2.01 /PERSON — SERVES 4 — EASE ★★☆☆☆ — PREP 25 MINS — OK TO FREEZE ❄ — GF

SWEET CHILLI CHICKEN

SAUCE

4 tablespoons **soft brown sugar**

2 tablespoons freshly grated **ginger**

1/2 x 190ml bottle **sweet chilli sauce**

4 tablespoons **mirin** or **white wine vinegar**

juice of 2 **limes**

1/2 mug (150ml) **water**

1 teaspoon **cornflour**

3 **chicken breasts**, cut into thin strips

1 1/2 mugs (375g) **basmati rice**

200g **mangetout**, cut into thin strips

1 tablespoon **olive oil**

1 **fat red chilli**, chopped

1 Mix together the sauce ingredients. Add the chicken strips and leave for 5 minutes.

2 Meanwhile, put the rice on to cook. Once it is cooked, put the mangetout on top and replace the pan lid. The mangetout will cook in the heat from the rice.

3 Heat the oil in a large frying pan or wok. Add the chicken, but not the sauce. Fry on a medium heat until the chicken is cooked; should take 4–5 minutes.

4 Add the sauce and bring to the boil. Simmer for 1 minute. Add the chilli now if you want to add a real kick.

5 Serve with the rice and mangetout.

🌀 COOK FOOLPROOF RICE: FOR 4 PEOPLE, PUT 3 MUGS BOILING WATER IN A PAN, ADD 1 1/2 MUGS BASMATI RICE. BRING TO THE BOIL. SIMMER GENTLY WITH A LID ON THE PAN FOR 10 MINUTES. THE WATER SHOULD BE ABSORBED AND THE RICE FLUFFY.

SAUSAGE & TROTTOLE PASTA

A brilliant weekday alternative to the normal 'Spag Bol'. The chilli is optional if you have younger children.

GLUTEN-FREE: use GF pasta, stock cube and sausages.

2 mugs (200g) **pasta** (we used Trottole)

1 tablespoon **olive oil**

1 **red onion**, chopped

2 cloves **garlic**, chopped

500g **sausages**

1 mug (300ml) **water**

1 **vegetable stock cube**

6 medium **tomatoes**, chopped

1 tablespoon **tomato purée**

1 **fat red chilli**, sliced

2 tablespoons freshly chopped **basil**

1 Cook the pasta in a pan of salted, boiling water. Drain and put to one side.

2 Heat the oil in a wok, or large frying pan. Add the onion and garlic and fry until the onion begins to soften.

3 Take the skins of the sausages and break up. Add to the pan and fry until they begin to brown.

4 Add the water, stock cube, tomatoes and tomato purée. Bring to the boil and then turn down to simmer for 5 minutes. Add the chilli, if you are using it, and season well with salt and pepper.

5 Combine the pasta with the sausage mixture. Sprinkle the basil over and serve.

CHICKEN & MUSHROOM CURRY WITH COCONUT MILK

This is super quick for a curry. Perfect for when you get in from work and need food on the table 'pronto'.

GLUTEN-FREE: use GF plain flour, curry paste and naan bread.

1 1/2 mugs (375g) **basmati rice**

1 tablespoon **olive oil**

1 **onion**, sliced

3 **chicken breasts**, cut into chunks

4 tablespoons **Korma curry paste**

1 tablespoon **plain flour**

400ml tin **coconut milk**

250g **mushrooms**, sliced

peshwari naan

1　Cook the rice. Once cooked, remove from the heat and leave with a lid on until needed.

2　Meanwhile, heat the oil in a large frying pan or wok. Add the onion and fry until it begins to soften.

3　Put the naan in the oven, see packet instructions.

4　Add the chicken to the frying pan and fry until no longer pink. Add the curry paste and mix well.

5　Add the flour and mix well.

6　Add the coconut milk and mushrooms. Bring to the boil and then turn down to simmer for 2 minutes.

BASIL & PARMESAN MEATBALLS

When making the meatballs, if you have a food processor, you can make the breadcrumbs, add the onion, then the basil and the rest of the meatball contents, blitzing between each addition.

GLUTEN-FREE: use GF bread, stock cubes and pasta.

TOMATO SAUCE

2 tablespoons **olive oil**

1 **onion**, finely chopped

1 clove **garlic**, chopped

6 medium **tomatoes**, chopped

2 tablespoons **tomato purée**

1 teaspoon **soft brown sugar**

1 mug (300ml) **water**

1 **vegetable stock cube**

3 sprigs **fresh rosemary**

MEATBALLS

500g **minced beef**

2 slices **wholemeal bread**, made into breadcrumbs

1 **onion**, chopped

1 tablespoon freshly chopped **basil**

½ mug (30g) grated **Parmesan**

1 **egg**, beaten

salt and **pepper**

2 tablespoons **olive oil**

400g **tagliatelle** or **spaghetti**

1 To make the sauce, heat the oil in a large saucepan, add the onions and garlic and fry until the onions begin to soften.

2 Add the rest of the sauce ingredients and bring to the boil. Turn down to simmer for 15 minutes. Take out the rosemary and blitz with a hand-held blender. If you do not have one, just leave as it is.

3 Combine together the beef, breadcrumbs, onion, basil, Parmesan, egg and salt and pepper in a large bowl. Make into about 24 meatballs.

4 Heat the oil in a frying pan and add the meatballs. Cook on a medium heat until they are browned on all sides and cooked through. This may take about 10 minutes.

5 Meanwhile, cook the tagliatelli; usually takes no more than 4 minutes.

PAPRIKA SAUSAGE SALAD

GLUTEN-FREE: use GF sausages.

8 **sausages**

2 teaspoons **paprika**

1 tablespoon **olive oil**

DRESSING

3 tablespoons **extra virgin olive oil**

2 tablespoons **cider vinegar**

1 tablespoon **runny honey**

salt and **pepper**

SALAD

250g **cherry tomatoes**, quartered

20 **black olives**

1 teaspoon **capers**, chopped

2 **cos lettuce**, sliced

8 **spring onions**, sliced

Parmesan cheese, shaved

1 Peel the skins off the sausages and break each one into 4 pieces; no need to roll into balls. Sprinkle the paprika onto a plate and add salt and pepper. Roll the sausage pieces in the mixture.

2 Heat the oil in a large frying pan and add the sausages. Fry until the pieces are browned and cooked through; it will take about 5 minutes.

3 Mix together the dressing ingredients.

4 Mix together the salad ingredients in a bowl. Add the dressing and mix together.

5 Serve with the sausages and Parmesan.

CASHEW NUT CHICKEN

GLUTEN-FREE: use GF stock cubes.

CASHEW NUT PASTE

1 **onion**, roughly chopped

2 tablespoons **tomato purée**

50g **cashew nuts**

1 tablespoon **garam masala**

2 cloves **garlic**

juice of 1/2 a **lemon**

1 teaspoon **ground turmeric**

1 mug (300ml) **water**

1 1/2 mugs (375g) **basmati rice**

50g **cashew nuts**

2 tablespoons **olive oil**

3 **chicken breasts**, cut into chunks

14 **ready-to-eat dried apricots**, roughly chopped

1 **chicken stock cube**

3 tablespoons **Greek yogurt**

3 tablespoons freshly chopped **coriander**

1 Put the ingredients for the nut paste in a food processor and blitz to form a paste. If you do not have a processor, simply chop everything very finely.

2 Cook the rice and then set to one side, with the lid on the pan, until needed.

3 Meanwhile, heat a wok and dry toast the second 50g cashew nuts, until lightly browned. Keep them moving in the pan, so they don't burn. Remove from the wok and leave to one side until needed.

4 Heat the oil in a wok, add the chicken breast and fry for 1 minute.

5 Add the nut paste, apricots, stock cube and simmer for 3–4 minutes until the chicken is cooked through. Season with salt and pepper.

6 Mix the coriander and yogurt together in a small bowl and serve with the chicken, rice and tooasted cashews.

🥘 COOK FOOLPROOF RICE: FOR 4 PEOPLE, PUT 3 MUGS BOILING WATER IN A PAN, ADD 1 1/2 MUGS BASMATI RICE. BRING TO THE BOIL. SIMMER GENTLY WITH A LID ON THE PAN FOR 10 MINUTES. THE WATER SHOULD BE ABSORBED AND THE RICE FLUFFY.

£ 1.23 /PERSON · SERVES 4 · EASE ★★☆☆☆ · PREP 25 MINS · GF OPTION · V OPTION

LEEK & TARRAGON RIGATONI

GLUTEN-FREE: use GF pasta and stock cubes.

VEGETARIAN OPTION: use Parmesan-style cheese.

2 mugs (200g) **Rigatoni**

50g **butter**, measure using packet

1 tablespoon **olive oil**

2 large **leeks**, sliced

250g **chestnut mushrooms**

2 tablespoons freshly chopped **tarragon**, or 1 teaspoon **dried tarragon**

300ml **single cream**

1 **vegetable stock cube**

¼ mug (15g) grated **Parmesan**

1 Put the pasta on to cook. Once cooked, drain and return to the pan, with a drizzle of olive oil, until needed.

2 Meanwhile, heat the butter and oil in a wok or large saucepan. Fry the leeks until soft and beginning to brown. Add the mushrooms and fry for a further 2 minutes.

3 Add the tarragon, cream, stock and cook for 2 minutes. Season to taste.

4 Stir in the pasta and the Parmesan.

SALMON & CORIANDER PATTIES WITH CRÈME FRAÎCHE RAITA

GLUTEN-FREE: use GF bread.

RAITA

3 tablespoons **crème fraîche**

¼ **cucumber**, grated

1 tablespoon freshly chopped **chives**

500g **salmon fillets**

2 slices **white bread**, made into breadcrumbs

2 teaspoons **capers**, chopped

2 tablespoons freshly chopped **coriander**

1 tablespoon **olive oil**

1 bag **salad leaves**

1 Mix the raita ingredients together and season to taste.

2 Put the salmon in a food processor and pulse a few times; no need to make the fish into a paste. If you don't have a processor, chop very finely.

3 Add the breadcrumbs, capers and coriander to the processor and pulse a couple of times. Season with salt and pepper.

4 Tip the mixture out onto a board and form into 8 patties.

5 Heat the oil in a frying pan and fry the patties for about 4 minutes on each side, on a medium heat.

6 Serve with the salad and raita.

QUICK CHICKEN & RED LENTIL CURRY

GLUTEN-FREE: use GF curry paste.

1 tablespoon **olive oil**

1 **onion**, sliced

3 **chicken breasts**, cut into chunks

2 tablespoons **Korma curry paste**

6 large **tomatoes**, chopped

1 mug (300ml) **water**

1/2 mug (125g) **red lentils**

100g **spinach**, roughly chopped

1 1/2 mugs (375g) **basmati rice**

4 tablespoons **Greek yogurt**

1   Heat the oil in a wok or large saucepan. Add the onions and fry until they begin to soften.

2   Add the chicken and fry until it is no longer pink.

3   Add the curry paste and cook for 1 minute.

4   Add the tomatoes, water and lentils. Bring to the boil, then turn down to simmer for 15 minutes.

5   Put the rice on to cook. Set to one side until needed.

6   Stir the spinach into the curry and cook for 30 seconds.

7   Serve with the rice and yogurt.

MARSALA MUSHROOMS WITH CREAMY POLENTA

You can get some excellent packs of mixed mushrooms (which work well in this dish) from most supermarkets. It is well worth splashing out a little, as the variation in the types of mushroom add different textures and flavours.

POLENTA

1 1/2 mugs (450ml) **milk**

1 clove **garlic**, finely chopped

1/2 mug (100g) **fine polenta**

1/2 mug (150ml) **double cream**

1/2 mug (30g) grated **Parmesan**

150g **mascarpone cheese**

50g **butter**, measure using packet

450g **mixed mushrooms**, e.g. porcini, girolles and chanterelles, roughly chopped

2 cloves **garlic**, chopped

1/4 mug (75ml) **Marsala wine**

2 tablespoons freshly chopped **basil**

1 To make the polenta, put the milk, garlic, polenta, cream and salt and pepper in a medium pan. Bring to the boil, stirring frequently. Turn down to simmer for 10 minutes, again stirring frequently. Add the Parmesan and mascarpone and mix well. Set to one side until needed.

2 Meanwhile, melt the butter in a large frying pan or wok. Add the mushrooms and garlic and fry gently for 2 minutes. Season well, add the Marsala wine and cook for 1 minute. Take off the heat and add the fresh basil.

3 Serve together.

KHEEMA ALOO

Kheema Aloo is a traditional South Asian dish with mince and potatoes, ginger and garlic. With my limited understanding of the Indian language, basically, 'kheema' means the minced meat and 'aloo' the potatoes.

1 tablespoon **olive oil**

4 **cardamom pods**

1 **cinnamon stick**

3 **cloves**

2 **onions**, chopped

500g **minced lamb**

2 teaspoons **garam masala**

1 **fat red chilli**, finely chopped

2 cloves **garlic**, finely chopped

1 tablespoon freshly grated **ginger**

2 medium **potatoes**, cut into small chunks

400g tin **chopped tomatoes**

1/2 mug (150ml) **water**

2 tablespoons freshly chopped **coriander**

1 1/2 mugs (375g) **basmati rice**

2 **naan bread**

1 Heat the oil in a wok or large frying pan. Add the cardamom pods, cinnamon stick and cloves and fry for 30 seconds, to release the flavours.

2 Add the onions and fry until they begin to soften.

3 Add the lamb to the pan and fry until it is no longer pink.

4 Add the garam masala, chilli, garlic and ginger and fry for another minute. Season well with salt and pepper.

5 Add the potatoes, tomatoes and water and bring to the boil. Turn down to simmer, with a lid on the pan, for 12–15 minutes until the potatoes are tender.

6 Cook the rice or naan.

7 Stir the coriander into the meat mixture and serve with the rice or naan bread.

HARISSA & TUNA POTATO SALAD

The harissa dressing really brings this salad alive; rich and tomatoey, with a spicy kick for good measure.

500g **new potatoes**, cut into chunks

200g **green beans**, trimmed

1 mug (150g) **frozen soya beans**, defrosted

2 x 185g tins **tuna**, drained and flaked

1/2 bag **rocket leaves**

8 **anchovies**, sliced lengthways

DRESSING

2 teaspoons **harissa paste**

juice of a **lemon**

2 tablespoons **extra virgin olive oil**

1 teaspoon **honey**

1 Put the potatoes in a pan of salted, boiling water, bring to the boil and then simmer for 5 minutes. Add the green beans and soya beans and simmer for a further 5 minutes. Drain and return to the pan.

2 Gently stir in the flaked tuna. Serve on a bed of rocket leaves. Put a few sliced anchovies on each plate of salad.

3 Mix together the dressing ingredients and drizzle over.

SCAN ME

🌏 **LOOKING FOR A CHEAP AND CHEERFUL DISH? TRY:**
WWW.NOSHBOOKS.COM/TUNA-HASH

WARM ASIAN SALMON SALAD

This is a delicious, crunchy, fresh tasting salad, which is full of barely cooked vegetables and healthy salmon. So, not only can you enjoy eating it, you can also feel totally guilt-free at the same time.

GLUTEN-FREE: make sure the soy and fish sauce are gluten-free.

2/3 mug (150g) **basmati rice**

2 **pak choi**, finely sliced

100g **sugar snaps** or **mangetout**, halved

3 tablespoons **toasted sesame oil**

4 **salmon fillets**

3 tablespoons **sesame seeds**

6 **spring onions**, sliced

3 tablespoons **dark soy sauce**

2 tablespoons **Thai fish sauce**

juice of a **lime**

1 tablespoon **runny honey**

200g **beansprouts**

2 tablespoons freshly chopped **coriander**

1 Add the rice to 1 1/3 mugs of boiling water and simmer gently, with a lid on the pan, for 10 minutes. Take the pan off the heat and add the pak choi and sugar snaps. Replace the lid and leave to steam.

2 Heat the sesame oil in a large frying pan and fry the salmon, on a medium heat, until browned on both sides and cooked through.

3 Add the sesame seeds and spring onions and cook gently until they begin to brown.

4 Add the soy, fish sauce, lime and honey. Cook on a low heat for 30 seconds, being careful not to burn the honey.

5 Take the fish out and add the beansprouts, cooked rice, sugar snaps, pak choi and coriander and heat through for 1 minute.

6 Flake the fish and gently stir into the rice mix. Serve immediately.

SAUSAGE & BEAN SOUP

This is a hearty soup, full of goodness. A meal in one pot.

GLUTEN-FREE: make sure the sausages and stock are gluten-free.

8 **sausages**

1 tablespoon **olive oil**

1 **onion**, sliced

3 **celery sticks**, thinly sliced

2 cloves **garlic**, finely chopped

500g **passata**

1 **chicken stock cube**

2 mugs (600ml) **water**

400g tin **cannellini beans**, drained and rinsed

100g **spinach**, roughly chopped

1 Cut the sausage skins lengthways and peel off the skins. Squeeze each one into 6 pieces. Heat the oil in a large saucepan pan or wok. Fry the sausages until they are browned on all sides. Remove from the pan.

2 Add the onion, celery and garlic to the pan and fry until everything is lightly browned.

3 Add the passata, stock, water and beans. Return the sausages to the pan and season well with salt and pepper. Bring to the boil and then simmer for 5 minutes.

4 Take off the heat and add the spinach to the pan. Stir together and the spinach will wilt.

ITALIAN COD & BEAN STEW

Italian fish stew with a hint of spice. Find some good crusty bread to serve with this dish.

GLUTEN-FREE: make sure the fish stock cubes are gluten-free.

1 tablespoon **olive oil**

1 **red pepper**, chopped

4 slices **streaky bacon**, chopped

6 **spring onions**, chopped

6 medium **tomatoes**, roughly chopped

2 cloves **garlic**, finely chopped

2 teaspoons **paprika**

1 pinch **saffron** threads

400g tin **cannellini beans**, drained and rinsed

1 mug (300ml) **water**

1 **fish stock cube**

4 **cod steaks**, cut into chunks

2 tablespoons freshly chopped **coriander**

1 **crusty baguette**

1 Heat the oil in a large frying pan or wok. Add the pepper and bacon and fry until it begins to brown. Season well with salt and pepper.

2 Add the spring onions, tomatoes and garlic and fry for 1 minute.

3 Add the paprika, saffron, beans, water and stock and bring to the boil. Add the cod, stir in carefully, and simmer gently for 3-4 minutes, or until the fish is cooked.

4 Add the chopped coriander and stir in. Serve with some crusty bread.

MUSHROOM & BACON TAGLIATELLE

GLUTEN-FREE: use GF pasta.

4 bunches **tagliatelle**

250g **streaky bacon**

1 tablespoon **olive oil**

1 **yellow/orange pepper**, cut into small chunks

2 cloves **garlic**, finely chopped

1 bunch **spring onions**, chopped

250g **chestnut mushrooms**, sliced

300ml **Greek yogurt**

¼ mug (50g) **pine nuts**

2 tablespoons freshly chopped **basil**

1 Put the pasta on to cook. Once cooked, drain and return to the pan until needed.

2 Meanwhile, fry or grill the bacon until browned. Cut into bite-sized pieces.

3 Heat the oil in a large frying pan, or wok, and add the peppers and garlic. Fry for 2-3 minutes until the peppers begin to brown. Add the mushrooms and spring onions and fry for 1 minute.

4 Add the yogurt and pine nuts and heat through.

5 Add the bacon, basil and pasta to the pan and mix together. Season well.

NEVER WAIT FOR WATER TO BOIL IN A PAN. BOIL THE WATER IN THE KETTLE FIRST.

ALMONDS & APRICOT CHICKEN TAGINE

Tagines typically sit in the oven for long periods of time which, if you have got the time, is great. Most people want things a little quicker though, so we wanted to try and get the flavour without all that time. This one is packed with fruity flavours and the unmistakable spices of a tagine, in a fraction of the time.

1 mug (200g) **couscous**

2 mugs (600ml) **boiling water**

1 **vegetable stock cube**

2 tablespoons freshly chopped **coriander**

1 tablespoon **olive oil**

1 large **onion**, sliced

2 cloves **garlic**, finely chopped

3 **chicken breasts**, cut into chunks

1 teaspoon **ground cinnamon**

1 **cinnamon stick**

1 teaspoon **ground coriander**

1/2 teaspoon **paprika**

1 mug (150g) **ready-to-eat dried apricots**, roughly chopped

250g **mushrooms**, sliced

1 mug (175g) **sultanas**

1 1/2 mugs (450ml) **water**

1 **chicken stock cube**

2 teaspoons **cornflour**

1 tablespoon freshly chopped **coriander**

50g **flaked almonds**

1 Put the couscous in a large bowl, add the boiling water and stock cube and stir well, to dissolve the stock. Cover the bowl with a plate, or cling film, and leave to one side for at least 4 minutes. Just before serving, add the fresh coriander.

2 Heat the oil in a large frying pan or wok. Add the onions and garlic and fry until they begin to soften.

3 Add the chicken and fry until no longer pink.

4 Add the cinnamon, cinnamon stick, ground coriander, paprika, apricots, mushrooms, sultanas, water and stock. Bring to the boil and turn down to simmer for 10 minutes.

5 Mix the cornflour with a little water and add to the pan. This should thicken the sauce.

6 Just before serving, stir in the fresh coriander. Serve with the couscous and sprinkle over the flaked almonds.

MEATBALL PASTA BAKE

GLUTEN-FREE: use GF bread, pasta and stock cubes.

3 mugs (300g) **pasta** (we used colourful Fusilloni)

MEATBALLS

500g **minced beef**

1 **egg**

1 teaspoon **dried oregano**

2 slices **bread**, made into breadcrumbs

salt and **pepper**

1 tablespoon **olive oil**

SAUCE

1 **onion**, chopped

2 **ready-roasted red peppers**, roughly chopped

500g **passata**

1/2 mug (150ml) **water**

1 **beef stock cube**

200g **mozzarella cheese**

1 tablespoon freshly chopped **thyme leaves**

1 Cook the pasta in a pan of salted, boiling water. Drain and return to the pan until needed.

2 Meanwhile, make the meatballs. Mix the mince, egg, oregano and 1/2 the breadcrumbs together in a bowl. Season well with salt and pepper. Divide into 24 pieces and form the meatballs.

3 Heat the oil in a large frying pan, or wok, and fry the meatballs until they are cooked through and browned on all sides. Place in the casserole dish.

4 To make the sauce, add the onions to the pan and fry until they begin to soften.

5 Add the peppers, passata, water and stock cube and simmer for 2 minutes.

6 Mix in the drained pasta and pour into the casserole dish with the meatballs.

7 Preheat the grill.

8 Pull apart the mozzarella and spread over the top, along with the thyme. Sprinkle over the rest of the breadcrumbs. Place under the grill for 5 minutes. The cheese should be bubbling and the breadcrumbs browned.

SCAN ME

🌐 **YOU CAN'T BEAT A PASTA BAKE. HERE IS ANOTHER:**
WWW.NOSHBOOKS.COM/TUNA-BAKE

QUICK BEEF & YORKSHIRE PUDDING

This is Ron's Yorkshire Pudding recipe. Even though he does not originate from Yorkshire, and I do, he makes the best 'Yorkshires' in our house. This makes a fun meal to share.

YORKSHIRE PUDDING

1 mug (200g) **plain flour**

5 **eggs**

5 tablespoons **milk**

pinch of **salt**

2 tablespoons **Trex** or **White Flora**

BEEF

1 tablespoon **olive oil**

1 **red onion**, chopped

750g **minced beef**

2 tablespoons **plain flour**

2 mugs (600ml) **water**

2 **beef stock cubes**

4 **carrots**, cut into small chunks

2 sprigs **rosemary**

green veg

1 Preheat the oven to 250°C fan/270°C/gas 9. Leave only one shelf in the oven to allow the pudding plenty of room to rise.

2 Mix the Yorkshire Pudding ingredients to a smooth consistency. Add 5 tablespoons of water, enough to make the mixture as thick as single cream. Store in a cool place until needed.

3 On the hob, heat the Trex in a large hob to oven casserole dish, preferably one which is wide and shallow. When the fat begins to smoke a little, add the beaten-up Yorkshire pudding mix. Leave on a high heat and do not stir. Once the Yorkshire begins to slightly brown around the edges carefully transfer into the hot oven and bake for about 20 minutes. The pudding should rise and be quite brown. Don't open the oven until you are sure it is done.

4 Meanwhile, prepare the beef. Heat the oil in a large frying pan or wok, add the onions and fry until they begin to soften. Add the mince and fry until it is no longer pink.

5 Add the flour and mix well. Add the rest of the ingredients and season with salt and pepper. Bring to the boil and then turn down to simmer for 15 minutes.

6 Meanwhile, put the green veg on to cook.

CHORIZO PASTA BAKE

GLUTEN-FREE: use GF chorizo and pasta.

2 tablespoons **olive oil**

2 **red peppers**, cut into chunks

2 **courgettes**, cut into chunks

300g **chorizo sausage**, cut into chunks

2 mugs (200g) **pasta** (we used Casarecce)

6 medium **tomatoes**, chopped

1/2 mug (150ml) **water**

1 tablespoon **tomato purée**

1 clove **garlic**, finely chopped

1 tablespoon freshly chopped **basil**

15 **olives**, halved

1 mug (40g) grated **Cheddar cheese**

1 Heat the oil in a wok and add the peppers and courgettes. Fry until they begin to brown. Add the chorizo and fry until it begins to brown.

2 Cook the pasta in a pan of salted, boiling water. Drain and set to one side until needed.

3 Add the tomatoes, water, tomato purée, garlic and basil to the wok. Bring to the boil and then turn down to simmer for 5 minutes.

4 Preheat the grill.

5 Add the pasta, basil and olives to the wok. Mix everything and then pour into a flameproof casserole dish. Sprinkle the cheese over the top and place under the grill for about 5 minutes to brown the top.

🌐 **SEE ANOTHER PASTA BAKE ONLINE: WWW.NOSHBOOKS.COM/PASTA-BAKE**

SCAN ME

LAMB & CHILLI GRATINATA

GLUTEN-FREE: use GF pasta, stock cube and breadcrumbs.

2 mugs (200g) **pasta** (we used Penne)

1 tablespoon **olive oil**

1 **onion**, chopped

500g **minced lamb**

2 cloves **garlic**, finely chopped

150g **mushrooms**, sliced

1/2 **red chilli**, deseeded and chopped

500g **passata**

1/2 mug (150ml) **water**

1 **lamb stock cube**

75g **olives**, about 20

100g **spinach**, roughly chopped

2 slices **wholemeal bread** made into breadcrumbs

200g **mozzarella cheese**, pulled apart

1 Preheat the oven to 180°C fan/200°C/gas 6. Grease a large casserole dish.

2 Cook the pasta in a pan of salted, boiling water. Drain, return to the pan and set to one side.

3 Meanwhile, heat the oil in a large frying pan, or wok, and fry the onions until they begin to soften.

4 Add the mince to the pan and fry until it is no longer pink.

5 Add the garlic, mushrooms, chilli, passata, water and stock, bring to the boil and then simmer for 5 minutes. Season well with salt and pepper.

6 Add the olives, spinach and pasta to the pan and mix together. Pour into the casserole dish.

7 Sprinkle the breadcrumbs over the top and then distribute the mozzarella over the top.

8 Place in the oven for 15–20 minutes or until the top is nicely browned.

GET OUT ALL THE INGREDIENTS BEFORE YOU START; IT MAKES COOKING A LOT CALMER.

MUSTARD CHICKEN & PANCETTA GRATIN

Quick and easy to make. You could exchange the pancetta for 8 rashers of chopped up, streaky bacon if you like.

5 medium **potatoes**, thinly sliced

2 tablespoons **olive oil**

1 **onion**, sliced

200g **pancetta lardons**

250g **mushrooms**, sliced

3 **chicken breasts**, cut into chunks

300ml **single cream**

2 tablespoons freshly chopped **thyme leaves**

1 tablespoon **wholegrain mustard**

1/2 mug (30g) grated **Parmesan**

1 Add the potatoes to a pan of salted, boiling water and simmer for 5 minutes until tender. Remove from the pan and set to one side until needed.

2 Heat the oil in a large frying pan, or wok, and fry the onion and pancetta until they begin to brown.

3 Add the mushrooms and chicken and fry until the chicken is cooked through. Season well with salt and pepper.

4 Preheat the grill.

5 Pour into a large casserole dish and arrange the cooked potatoes over the top.

6 Mix together the cream, thyme leaves and wholegrain mustard. Pour over the potatoes and sprinkle the Parmesan over the top.

7 Place under the grill for 5-8 minutes, or until the cheese has begun to brown.

FLORENTINE CHICKEN BAKE

Florentine dishes tend to have lots of spinach in them and are often topped with mozzarella, so this bake fits the brief nicely.

GLUTEN-FREE: use GF pasta, stock cubes and plain flour.

3 mugs (300g) **pasta** (we used Ziti)

1 tablespoon **olive oil**

3 **chicken breasts**, cut into chunks

2 tablespoons **plain flour**

1 mug (300ml) **water**

1 **chicken stock cube**

2 tablespoons **sun-dried tomato purée**

100g **Philadelphia cream cheese**

250g **spinach**, roughly chopped

250g **mozzarella cheese**

1/2 mug (30g) grated **Parmesan**

1 Preheat the grill.

2 Cook the pasta in a pan of salted, boiling water. Once cooked, drain and return to the pan.

3 Meanwhile, heat the oil in a large hob-to-oven saucepan or dish. Add the chicken breast and fry until no longer pink.

4 Add the flour and mix. Add the water, stock cube and tomato purée and bring to the boil, stirring frequently. Add the Philadelphia and stir on a low heat until it melts. Season with salt and pepper.

5 Add the spinach and cook until it wilts; about 1 minute. Add the cooked pasta and mix together.

6 Arrange the mozzarella over the top and then sprinkle over the Parmesan. Place under the grill for about 5 minutes, or until the cheese bubbles and browns.

CHICKEN, PANCETTA & LEEK BAKE

GLUTEN-FREE: use GF flour, pasta and bread.

SAUCE

50g **butter**, measure using packet

2 tablespoons **plain flour**

2 mugs (600ml) **milk**

1 teaspoon **mustard**

1 mug (75g) grated **Cheddar cheese**

2 mugs (200g) **pasta** (we used Fusilli)

1 tablespoon **olive oil**

125g pack **pancetta lardons**

3 medium **leeks**, sliced

2 large **chicken breasts**, cut into chunks

TOPPING

2 slices **white bread**, made into breadcrumbs

2 tablespoons freshly chopped **basil**

½ mug (30g) grated **Parmesan**

1   Make the sauce by melting the butter in a saucepan, add the flour and mix to a paste. Allow to bubble for 30 seconds, before adding the milk, mustard and cheese. Mix it together, bring to the boil and stir with a small whisk to prevent lumps forming. Leave to one side until needed.

2   Cook the pasta in a pan of salted, boiling water. Once cooked, drain and return to the pan.

3   Meanwhile, preheat the grill.

4   Heat the oil in a large saucepan or wok. Add the pancetta and cook until it begins to brown.

5   Add the leeks and cook until they begin to soften.

6   Add the chicken and cook for 2-3 minutes until cooked through.

7   Add the sauce and the pasta. Mix together and pour into a large casserole dish.

8   Mix the topping ingredients and sprinkle over the top. Place under the grill for about 5 minutes until browned.

LEEK & SALMON PIE

GLUTEN-FREE: use GF plain flour.

5 medium **potatoes**, cut into small chunks (no need to peel)

75g **butter**, measure using packet

2 medium **leeks**, sliced

2 tablespoons **plain flour**

1 1/2 mugs (450ml) **milk**

300ml **double cream**

4 **salmon steaks**, cut into chunks

1 mug (150g) **frozen peas**, defrosted

2 tablespoons freshly chopped **dill**

1/2 mug (30g) grated **Parmesan**

1 Preheat the oven to 180°C fan/200°C/gas 6. Grease a large casserole dish.

2 Put the potatoes in a pan of salted, boiling water and simmer for 10 minutes. Drain and return to the pan. Add 25g of the butter and shake the pan around to distribute.

3 Meanwhile, add another 25g of the butter to a large frying pan and fry the leeks until they begin to soften and brown. Put the leeks in the casserole dish, along with the defrosted peas.

4 Add the last 25g butter to the frying pan, along with the flour, and cook on a medium heat until the flour is absorbed. Add the milk and cream to the pan and gently bring to the boil, stirring all the time. Add the fish and dill to the sauce and cook, on a medium heat, for 2 minutes. The fish does not need to be cooked through, as it will go in the oven.

5 Pour the sauce and the fish into the casserole dish and mix with the leeks. Season well. Pile the potatoes on top and sprinkle the grated Parmesan over.

6 Place in the oven for 20 minutes. The top should be lightly browned.

CHORIZO BOULANGERIE

Super-quick to prepare, but needs a bit longer in the oven. This makes for an ideal mid-week dish when you get in from work and want to quickly throw something in the oven and then relax while it cooks.

GLUTEN-FREE: use GF chorizo and stock cubes.

5 medium **potatoes**, unpeeled and cut into 1cm slices

1 **onion**, sliced

250g **chestnut mushrooms**, sliced

200g **cubed chorizo**

½ mug (150ml) **hot water**

1 **vegetable stock cube**

½ mug (30g) grated **Parmesan**

1 Preheat the oven to 180°C fan/200°C/gas 6. Grease a medium casserole dish.

2 Place the potatoes, onions, mushrooms and chorizo in layers in the casserole dish.

3 Dissolve the stock cube in the water and pour over.

4 Sprinkle the grated Parmesan over the top and place in the oven for 45-50 minutes, until nicely browned.

CIDER PORK & BACON PIE WITH CAULIFLOWER & POTATO MASH

GLUTEN-FREE: use GF flour and stock cube.

5 medium **potatoes**, peeled and cut into chunks

1 small **cauliflower**, cut into small florets

3/4 mug (60g) grated **Cheddar cheese**

1 tablespoon **wholegrain mustard**

150g **streaky bacon**

1 **onion**, sliced

500g **minced pork**

2 **leeks**, sliced

1 tablespoon **plain flour**

1 mug (300ml) **cider**

1 **vegetable stock cube**

1 Preheat the oven to 200°C fan/220°C/gas 7. Grease a large casserole dish.

2 Put the potatoes and the cauliflower in a saucepan of salted, boiling water and simmer for 10 minutes. Drain and return to the pan. Add the cheese and mustard and mash together.

3 Meanwhile, fry the bacon in a large frying pan until it is crispy. Remove from the pan, cut into smaller pieces and set to one side until needed.

4 In the same frying pan, fry the onions until they become soft. Add the mince and fry until it is no longer pink.

5 Add the leeks and fry for 2 minutes.

6 Add the flour and stir well.

7 Add the cider and the stock cubes. Mix together, bring to the boil and season. Add the chopped bacon and pour into the casserole dish.

8 Put the mash on top. Place in the oven for 25-30 minutes, or until the top is browned.

TAGLIATELLE TUNA BAKE WITH MUSHROOM & BROCCOLI

Tuna bake is always a great, economic way to feed the family. This one is so tasty, looks good and also has some healthy veg incorporated.

GLUTEN-FREE: use GF pasta.

6 nests **tagliatelle**

1 small head **broccoli**, cut into florets

1 tablespoon **olive oil**

250g **mushrooms**, sliced

1 bunch **spring onions**, sliced

1 mug (150g) **frozen peas**, defrosted

200g **Philadelphia cheese with garlic and herbs**

100g **crème fraîche**

2 x 185g tins **tuna**, drained and flaked

1 mug (60g) grated **Parmesan**

1 Put the tagliatelle and broccoli into a large saucepan of salted, boiling water and simmer for 5 minutes. Drain and return to the pan.

2 Heat the oil in a wok and fry the mushrooms and spring onions for 1 minute.

3 Add the peas, Philadelphia and crème fraîche. Heat through gently and season well. Add the tuna and gently mix.

4 Add the drained pasta and broccoli and mix together.

5 Preheat the grill.

6 Pour into a large casserole dish. Sprinkle the cheese over the top and place under the grill for 5 minutes, or until the cheese begins to brown.

FRIENDS AROUND

When you have friends over, you want to make something a little special, but not be stuck in the kitchen all night while everyone else has fun. Here are some ideas that fit the bill. Some you can prepare beforehand, like 'Mango Chicken Salad'. Others, like 'Paprika Salmon', are really quick to finish off once your friends arrive.

BEEF STEAK SALAD

GLUTEN-FREE: use GF ciabatta.

2 tablespoons **mustard powder**

1 teaspoon freshly ground **black pepper**

3 **rump steaks**

1 tablespoon **olive oil**

2 tablespoons **runny honey**

SALAD

2 **little gem lettuces**, sliced

200g **radishes**, thinly sliced

2 large **carrots**, cut into thin strips, using a peeler

2 tablespoons **pine nuts**

DRESSING

2 tablepoons **extra virgin olive oil**

juice of a **lemon**

1 teaspoon **granulated sugar**

salt and **pepper**

1 tablespoon freshly chopped **basil**

1 tablespoon freshly chopped **parsley**

1 large **ciabatta**, cut in half horizontally

1 clove **garlic**, peeled, but not chopped

1 Put the mustard and pepper on a large plate and season with salt. Press the steaks into the mixture and rub it onto the meat. Leave to stand for 5 minutes.

2 Meanwhile, prepare the salad ingredients and mix together the dressing ingredients.

3 Grill the ciabatta. Once lightly browned, remove from the grill and rub the garlic lightly over the surface. Cut into chunks.

4 Heat the oil in a frying pan and fry the steaks, for 2 minutes each side, on a high heat. If you like well done steak, turn down the heat and fry for another 2 minutes each side. Remove from the heat and drizzle over the honey. Turn over in the pan to coat both sides with the honey. Remove from the pan and cut into thin strips.

5 Arrange the meal on a sharing platter, or board. Pour over the dressing and any excess juices from the pan or chopping board.

THAI PORK CURRY

GLUTEN-FREE: use GF curry paste and fish sauce.

1 tablespoon **toasted sesame oil**

3 **pork steaks**, cut into thin strips

6 **spring onions**, sliced

1 **red pepper**, cut into chunks

125g **mushrooms**, sliced

400ml tin **coconut milk**

2 tablespoons **Thai red curry paste**

1 tablespoon **fish sauce**

225g tin **bamboo shoots**, drained

1 teaspoon **soft brown sugar**

2 tablespoons freshly chopped **coriander**

2 x 300g packs **fresh rice noodles**

1 Heat the oil in a wok, or large frying pan. Add the pork and fry on a high heat for 2–3 minutes, or until it begins to brown. Remove from the pan. Set to one side until needed.

2 Add the onions, peppers and mushrooms to the pan and fry for 2–3 minutes, or until the peppers begin to brown.

3 Add the coconut milk, curry paste and fish sauce to the pan and bring to the boil.

4 Add the bamboo shoots, sugar and coriander to the pan, along with the pork, and simmer for 1 minute.

5 Put the rice noodles in a bowl and pour boiling water over them. Leave to stand for 1 minute and then drain. Serve with the curry.

TROUT FILLETS WITH BEETROOT SALAD

Beetroot is not your 'run-of-the-mill' ingredient, so this, along with the thinly sliced radish, makes for an excellent summer salad with a difference.

ALMOND SAUCE

4 tablespoons **soured cream**

2 tablespoons freshly chopped **basil**

1 tablespoon **extra virgin olive oil**

2 tablespoons **toasted flaked almonds**, roughly chopped

salt and **pepper**

DRESSING

2 tablespoons **extra virgin olive oil**

juice of a **lemon**

1/2 teaspoon **granulated sugar**

salt and **pepper**

1 tablespoon **olive oil**

400g **trout fillets**

1 bag **rocket salad**

3 **gherkins**, sliced

100g **radishes**, finely sliced

4 **cooked beetroot**, cut into sticks

1 Mix together the almond sauce ingredients and set to one side until needed.

2 Mix together the dressing ingredients.

3 Heat the tablespoon of olive oil in the frying pan and add the trout fillets. Fry on both sides; they will take only 2–3 minutes to cook through. Remove from the pan and take the skins off. Flake the fish gently.

4 Arrange the salad and trout on the plates. Drizzle over the dressing and serve with the almond cream.

SCAN ME

🌐 **WE HAVE GOT A BEAUTIFUL GOATS' CHEESE SALAD HERE: WWW.NOSHBOOKS.COM/GOATS-CHEESE**

LAMB CHOPS WITH PANCETTA SALAD & YOGURT DRESSING

GLUTEN-FREE: use GF bread.

DRESSING

juice of a **lemon**

1/2 mug (30g) grated **Parmesan**

4 tablespoons **Greek yogurt**

2 tablespoons freshly chopped **mint**

2 tablespoons **extra virgin olive oil**

salt and **pepper**

SALAD

1 tablespoon **olive oil**

2 slices **wholemeal bread**

100g sliced **pancetta** (you can use streaky bacon)

125g **cherry tomatoes**, halved

3 **ready-roasted red peppers** (from a jar), roughly chopped

1/2 bag **salad**

8 **small lamb chops**

1 Mix the dressing ingredients together.

2 To make the croutons, heat the oil in a frying pan and fry the bread until it is brown on both sides. Take out of the pan and cut into small squares.

3 Fry the pancetta lightly; don't make it too crisp. Remove from the pan and cut into bite-sized pieces.

4 Mix all the salad ingredients together.

5 Heat a little oil in a frying pan and fry the lamb chops for 2 minutes each side. If you have larger, or thicker, chops, you will need to fry for a little longer. Season well.

6 Serve everything together.

MANGO CHICKEN SALAD

Super quick and easy recipe. The curry paste is not too spicy for children to try. If they are all grown up, then you can add more spice to taste, but not too much, or you will drown the other more subtle flavours.

GLUTEN-FREE: use GF curry paste.

3 **chicken breasts**, cut into strips
1 tablespoon **mild curry paste**
juice of a **lemon**
1 tablespoon **olive oil**

DRESSING
½ mug (150ml) **Greek yogurt**
1 tablespoon **mango chutney**

100g **watercress**
½ **cucumber**, cut into thin strips
6 **spring onions**, sliced
1 medium **Cos lettuce**, sliced
1 ripe **mango**, peeled and sliced

1 Put the chicken breast pieces in a bowl and add the curry paste and lemon juice. Mix together and leave for 10 minutes.

2 Meanwhile, mix together the dressing ingredients and set aside until needed.

3 Prepare the salad ingredients and divide between the plates.

4 Heat the oil in a large frying pan and fry the chicken pieces on a medium heat, taking care not to burn the curry paste. They should take no longer than 5 minutes to cook through. Check one of the thickest pieces to make sure.

5 Serve on the salad with the dressing drizzled over.

SCAN ME

 LIKE SWEET CHICKEN DISHES? HERE'S ANOTHER ONE:
WWW.NOSHBOOKS.COM/SWEETNSOUR

KOFTAS FROM KASHMIR

GLUTEN-FREE: use GF plain flour.

SPICE MIX

2 teaspoons **ground cumin**

2 teaspoons **ground coriander**

2 teaspoons **garam masala**

1/2 teaspoon **hot chilli powder**

1/2 teaspoon **ground turmeric**

KOFTAS

500g **minced lamb**

4 cloves **garlic**, finely chopped

12 **ready-to-eat dried apricots**, chopped

2 tablespoons freshly grated **ginger**

2 tablespoons **Greek yogurt**

2 tablespoons **plain flour**

25g **butter**, measure using packet

1 large **onion**, chopped

2 tablespoons **milk powder**

3 tablespoons **ground almonds**

2 teaspoons **granulated sugar**

2 mugs (600ml) **hot water**

1 1/2 mugs (375g) **basmati rice**

1 tablespoon freshly chopped **coriander**

1 Combine the spice mix in a small bowl.

2 In a large bowl, mix together the kofta ingredients, along with half of the spice mix. Season with salt and pepper. Roll the mixture into 20 small balls and dust with the flour.

3 Heat the butter in a large pan and add the onion. Once browned, turn down the heat and add the rest of the spice mix. Stir for about 30 seconds.

4 Add the remaining ingredients (excluding the rice and coriander), season with salt and pepper, and bring to the boil.

5 Add the koftas to the pan, bring back to the boil and turn down to simmer gently, with a lid on, for 10 minutes. After 5 minutes, check and gently turn the koftas.

6 Put the rice on to cook. Once cooked, leave with a lid on to keep warm until ready to serve.

7 Remove the lid from the koftas and simmer for 5 minutes until the sauce thickens. Serve with the rice.

SOUTHERN FRIED CHICKEN WITH POLENTA CHIPS

GLUTEN-FREE: use GF plain flour.

500g **ready-made polenta**

2 tablespoons **olive oil**

SAUCE

2 tablespoons **mayo**

2 tablespoons **Greek yogurt**

juice of a **lemon**

1 tablespoon **runny honey**

4 teaspoons **dried oregano**

2 teaspoons **paprika**

1 teaspoon **chilli powder**

2 teaspoons **dried mustard**

½ mug (100g) **plain flour**

2 tablespoons **runny honey**

juice of a **lemon**

3 **chicken breasts**, cut into strips

1 Preheat the oven, 200°C fan/220°C/gas 7.

2 Cut the polenta into chips. Put on two baking trays, drizzle with oil and season with salt and pepper. Carefully mix together to make sure everything is coated. Place in the oven for 30–40 minutes.

3 Mix together the sauce ingredients and set to one side until needed.

4 Put the oregano, paprika, chilli powder, mustard, flour and salt and pepper in a bowl. Put the honey and lemon in another bowl. Mix the honey and lemon together in a bowl. Dip the chicken pieces, first in the honey mix, and then in the spice mix. Try to attach as much as possible to the chicken.

5 Heat the oil in a large frying pan and fry the chicken for 2–3 minutes each side. The outside should be nicely browned and the inside cooked through.

6 Serve with the polenta chips and the sauce.

CHILLI CASHEW CHICKEN WITH HOISIN SAUCE & BAMBOO SHOOTS

Really simple, tasty dish, which most older children should love. Much less expensive that a Chinese takeaway. The longer you simmer the chilli, the hotter the dish will be.

GLUTEN-FREE: use GF hoisin and stock cubes.

1 1/2 mugs (375g) **basmati rice**

2 mugs (600ml) **water**

1 **chicken stock cube**

2 **carrots**, cut into thin sticks

250g tin **bamboo shoots**, drained and rinsed

3 medium **chicken breasts**, cut into thin strips

1/2 x 290g jar **hoisin sauce**

1 tablespoon **cornflour** mixed into 2 tablespoons **water**

3/4 mug (135g) **cashew nuts**

6 **spring onions**, sliced

1 **fat red chilli**, chopped

1 Cook the rice. Once cooked, leave to one side.

2 Meanwhile, heat the water and the chicken stock in a wok, add the carrots and simmer for 5 minutes.

3 Add the bamboo shoots and simmer for 3 minutes.

4 Add the chicken and simmer until the meat is no longer pink. Check the thickest piece.

5 Add the rest of the ingredients, bring to the boil and simmer for one minute.

6 Serve with the rice.

COOK FOOLPROOF RICE: FOR 4 PEOPLE, PUT 3 MUGS BOILING WATER IN A PAN, ADD 1 1/2 MUGS BASMATI RICE. BRING TO THE BOIL. SIMMER GENTLY WITH A LID ON THE PAN FOR 10 MINUTES. THE WATER SHOULD BE ABSORBED AND THE RICE FLUFFY.

SOY SALMON WITH WASABI MASH & PAK CHOI

GLUTEN-FREE: use GF soy.

MARINADE

4 tablespoons **soy sauce**

2 tablespoons **toasted sesame oil**

3 tablespoons **maple syrup**

juice of 2 **limes**

4 **salmon fillets**
(approx 500g total)

MASH

4 medium **potatoes**, peeled and cut into chunks

¼ mug (75ml) **double cream**

4 **spring onions**, chopped

1 teaspoon **wasabi paste**

1 tablespoon **toasted sesame seeds**

4 **pak choi**, sliced

1 Mix together the marinade ingredients and add the salmon.

2 Cover and leave for 10 minutes.

3 Whilst the salmon is marinading, simmer the potatoes in salted, boiling water for 10 minutes. Drain and return to the pan. Add the rest of the mash ingredients and mash together. Put a lid on the pan and set to one side until needed.

4 On medium heat, put a tablespoon of sesame oil in a frying pan. Remove the salmon from the marinade (keep the marinade for later) and fry the salmon until cooked through, turning once. It should take about 5 minutes, depending on the thickness of the fish.

5 Take the fish out of the pan, add the marinade to the pan, simmer for 1 minute and then remove from the heat.

6 In a large frying pan, or wok, heat another tablespoon of sesame oil. Add the pak choi and fry for 30 seconds. Add 1 tablespoon water, put a lid on the pan, and cook for a further 1 minute. Season.

7 Serve the salmon on top of the mash, with the pak choi to one side. Pour the sauce over. Sprinkle over with sesame seeds.

SEARED TUNA WITH ANCHOVY DRESSING

You can watch the tuna cooking as the sides turn from pink to white. Do not allow it to cook right through. Tuna will continue to cook even when taken out of the pan. If you cook it too much, it will go dry. Leave it a little rare in the middle (see photo).

GLUTEN-FREE: use GF bread.

DRESSING

4 **anchovies**, finely chopped

juice of a **lemon**

3 tablespoons **mayo**

2 tablespoons **extra virgin olive oil**

SALAD

2 **little gem lettuces**, chopped

1/2 **cucumber**, cut into sticks

4 **spring onions**, sliced lengthways

1 **egg**

2 slices **wholemeal bread**, made into breadcrumbs

zest of a **lemon**

2 tablespoons freshly chopped **basil**

4 fresh **tuna steaks**

2 tablespoons **olive oil**

1 Mix together the dressing ingredients and season. Prepare the salad.

2 Beat the egg in a small bowl. Mix together the breadcrumbs, lemon zest, basil and then season and put on a plate. Dip the tuna steaks into the egg and then press into the mixture.

3 Heat the oil in a large frying pan and fry the tuna steaks until each side is browned, but still rare in the centre.

4 Cut each steak into 3 or 4 and serve on top of the salad. Drizzle over the dressing.

PORK TACOS WITH A HARICOT BEAN SALSA

GLUTEN-FREE: use GF tacos.

BEAN SALSA

1 tablespoon **extra virgin olive oil**

6 medium **tomatoes**, chopped

2 cloves **garlic**, finely chopped

400g tin **haricot beans**, drained and rinsed

2 tablespoons freshly chopped **basil**

2 tablespoons **tomato purée**

1/2 mug (150ml) **water**

1 **fat red chilli**, finely chopped

4 **pork steaks**

1 tablespoon **paprika**

1 tablespoon **ground coriander**

1 tablespoon **olive oil**

2 **little gem lettuces**

8 **taco shells**

DRESSING

4 tablespoons **Greek yogurt**

juice of 1/2 **lemon**

2 tablespoons freshly chopped **coriander**

1 Heat the oil in a medium-sized saucepan. Add the tomatoes and garlic and fry for 2 minutes. Add the rest of the salsa ingredients, apart from the basil, and bring to the boil. Simmer for 2 minutes. Add the basil and set to one side until needed.

2 Put the paprika, ground coriander and some salt and pepper on a large plate. Press the pork steaks into the spice mixture. Rub the spices in.

3 Preheat the oven to 180°C fan/200°C/gas 6. Put the tacos on a baking sheet and heat in the oven for 2 minutes.

4 Heat the oil in a large frying pan and add the steaks. Fry for 2 minutes each side. If the steaks are thicker, fry for 1 minute longer each side. The outsides should be dark and crunchy and the insides must be cooked through. Check the thickest. Remove from the pan and slice into thin strips.

5 Mix together the dressing ingredients.

6 Arrange the ingredients in the taco shells and enjoy. Be warned, you will get messy eating them!

BEIJING-STYLE CRISPY CHICKEN PANCAKES

These Chinese pancakes may be tricky to get a hold of in all supermarkets. If your local one does not stock them, have a look around to see if there is a Chinese supermarket near you.

3 **chicken breasts**

4 tablespoons **hoisin sauce**

1 tablespoon **olive oil**

12 **Chinese pancakes**

1/2 **cucumber**, cut into sticks

12 **spring onions**, thinly sliced, lengthways

4 tablespoons **hoisin sauce**

1 tablespoon **water**

1 Put the chicken breasts between sheets of cling film and give them a 'bit of a bash' with a rolling pin to flatten them. Pour over the 4 tablespoons of hoisin and spread it over the chicken.

2 Heat the oil in a large frying pan and fry the chicken breasts for 2 minutes each side; the outsides should be browned and crispy. Check that they are cooked through.

3 Take out of the pan and cut into thin strips.

4 Heat the pancakes as per instructions on the packet.

5 Serve the slices of chicken with the pancakes, cucumber, onions and hoisin sauce.

PAPRIKA SALMON WITH SOY & HONEY

GLUTEN-FREE: make sure soy sauce is gluten-free.

1 mug (250g) **basmati rice**

2 mugs (600ml) **boiling water**

1 teaspoon **pilau rice seasoning** (optional)

2 **pak choi**, chopped

1 tablespoon **paprika**

4 **salmon steaks**

2 tablespoon **toasted sesame oil**

3 tablespoons **soy sauce**

3 tablespoons **runny honey**

1 Put the rice, water and pilau rice seasoning in a large saucepan. Simmer with a lid on the pan, for 8 minutes. Add the pak choi and return the lid to the pan. Cook for 2 minutes. Remove from the heat, mix together, replace the lid, and set aside until needed.

2 Put the paprika on a plate and press the salmon steaks into it.

3 Heat the oil in a frying pan and fry the salmon gently, so as not to burn the paprika. Once the salmon is cooked through, add the soy and honey to the pan and allow to simmer for 1 minute.

4 Serve the flaked fish on top of the rice and drizzle over the sauce.

CHICKEN IN BLACK BEAN SAUCE

GLUTEN-FREE: Use GF stock cubes, soy and black bean sauce.

1 1/2 mugs (375g) **basmati rice**

1 tablespoon **olive oil**

3 **chicken breasts**, cut into chunks

1 bunch **spring onions**, chopped

6 **mushrooms**, sliced

1 **fat red chilli**, chopped

1/2 mug (150ml) **water**

1 **chicken stock cube**

1 teaspoon **cornflour**

1 tablespoon **dark soy sauce**

1/2 x 195g bottle **black bean sauce**

1 Put the rice on to cook. Once cooked, leave the lid on the pan and set to one side until needed.

2 Heat the oil in a large frying pan, or wok. Add the chicken and fry until it is no longer pink.

3 Add the spring onions, mushrooms and chilli and fry for 1 minute.

4 Mix together the water, stock cube, cornflour, soy and black bean sauce. Add to the pan and bring to the boil. The sauce should thicken.

5 Serve with the rice.

🐾 COOK FOOLPROOF RICE: FOR 4 PEOPLE, PUT 3 MUGS BOILING WATER IN A PAN, ADD 1 1/2 MUGS BASMATI RICE. BRING TO THE BOIL. SIMMER GENTLY WITH A LID ON THE PAN FOR 10 MINUTES. THE WATER SHOULD BE ABSORBED AND THE RICE FLUFFY.

PAN ROASTED MARSALA CHICKEN WITH PARSNIP MASH

GLUTEN-FREE: use GF plain flour.

2 medium **potatoes**, peeled and cut into chunks

2 medium **parsnips**, peeled and cut into chunks

25g **butter**, measure using packet

1 tablespoon **olive oil**

2 **chicken breasts**

125g **chestnut mushrooms**, sliced

1/2 mug (150ml) **Marsala wine**

1 teaspoon **plain flour**

10g softened **butter**, measure using packet

220g **green beans**

1   Put the potatoes and the parsnips in a pan of boiling water and simmer for 10–12 minutes, or until the veg is tender. Drain and return to the pan. Add the 25g butter, season well with salt and pepper, and mash. Put a lid on the pan and set to one side.

2   Meanwhile heat the oil in a frying pan. Add the chicken breasts and season well with salt and pepper. Fry on each side for 2 minutes on a high heat. Turn down the heat and fry, with a lid on the pan, for 3–4 minutes on each side (depending on the thickness of the chicken).

3   Remove the chicken from the pan and slice. Add the mushrooms to the pan. Fry for 1 minute, add the Marsala and season. Simmer for 2–3 minutes.

4   Mix together the flour and softened butter, add to the pan and stir into the sauce. Simmer until it thickens slightly.

5   Meanwhile, put the beans in a pan of salted, boiling water and simmer for 5 minutes.

6   Serve the mash, chicken breast, sauce and beans.

PAN-FRIED CHICKEN WITH LIME & COCONUT SAUCE

GLUTEN-FREE: use GF stock cubes and fish sauce.

1 ½ mugs (375g) **basmati rice**

1 teaspoon **pilau rice seasoning** (optional)

2 tablespoons freshly chopped **coriander**

1 tablespoon **toasted sesame oil**

3 **chicken breasts**

LIME AND COCONUT SAUCE

1 tablespoon **toasted sesame oil**

1 clove **garlic**, chopped

2 tablespoons freshly grated **ginger**

juice of a **lime**

1 **chicken stock cube**

2 teaspoons **fish sauce**

1 teaspoon **granulated sugar**

400ml tin **coconut milk**

1 tablespoon **toasted sesame oil**

4 **pak choi**, sliced

1 Put the rice on to cook in 3 mugs of boiling water. Add the pilau rice seasoning and simmer, with a lid on the pan, for 10 minutes. Just before you serve the rice, add the chopped coriander.

2 Heat the oil in a frying pan and add the chicken breasts. Season well. Cook on a fairly high heat for 2 minutes each side. Turn the heat down to medium and cook for a further 4 minutes each side, with a lid on the pan. If the chicken breasts are really small, then cook for less time. Remove from the pan and set to one side until needed.

3 To make the sauce, heat the toasted sesame oil in a small saucepan and gently fry the garlic and ginger. Add the rest of the sauce ingredients, season and simmer gently for 5–6 minutes.

4 Heat the other tablespoon of toasted sesame oil in the frying pan and stir-fry the pak choi for 1 minute or until it begins to wilt slightly; it needs to be quite 'al dente'.

SCAN ME

🌐 **LIKE SPICY CHICKEN? WHY NOT TRY THIS RECIPE:**
WWW.NOSHBOOKS.COM/SPICED-CHICKEN

PEPPERED PORK WITH APPLE & BLUE CHEESE SALAD

Pork and apples are always a great duo and the addition of the blue cheese is a lovely complement to the more familiar combination.

DRESSING

75g **blue cheese**

2 tablespoons **extra virgin olive oil**

4 tablespoons **Greek yogurt**

juice of a **lemon**

salt and **pepper**

1 tablespoon freshly ground **black pepper**

4 **pork steaks**

1 tablespoon **olive oil**

SALAD

1 bag **rocket leaves**

1/2 **cucumber**, cut into sticks

4 **spring onions**, cut into thin strips

2 **Golden Delicious apples**, cut into thin sticks

1 Mix together the dressing ingredients and blend with a hand-held blender, if you have one, otherwise, squash the cheese with a fork. It doesn't matter if the dressing is a bit chunky.

2 Put the ground pepper on a plate and press the pork steaks into it to evenly coat them. Season with the salt. Heat the oil in a frying pan and fry the pork steaks for about 2 minutes each side, or more if they are thicker steaks. Remove from the pan and set to one side until needed.

3 Meanwhile, mix the salad ingredients together in a bowl. Divide between the plates and drizzle over the dressing. Cut the pork into strips and place on the top and serve.

£ 2.18 /PERSON · SERVES 4 · EASE ★★★☆☆ · PREP 30 MINS · GF OPTION

SWEET & SOUR SPICY COD

GLUTEN-FREE: make sure the soy sauce is gluten-free.

MASH

4 medium **potatoes**, cut into chunks

1 small **broccoli**, cut into florets

2 mugs (300g) **frozen peas**, defrosted

1 tablespoon freshly chopped **mint**

50g **butter**, measure using packet

2 tablespoons **olive oil**

4 **cod steaks**

SAUCE

2 cloves **garlic**, finely chopped

1 **fat red chilli**, cut into rings

3 tablespoons **red wine vinegar**

1 tablespoon **soft brown sugar**

4 tablespoons **soy sauce**

4 tablespoons **water** + 1 teaspoon **cornflour**

1 Put the potatoes in a pan of salted, boiling water, simmer for 5 minutes with the lid on, and then add the broccoli. After a further five minutes, add the defrosted peas and simmer for 2 minutes. Drain and return to the pan. Add the mint and the butter and mash slightly, leaving things a bit chunky. Set to one side until needed.

2 Heat the oil in a large frying pan and add the cod. Fry on a medium heat until lightly browned on each side and cooked through. Remove from the pan and set to one side.

3 Add the garlic and chillies to the pan and fry for 30 seconds.

4 In a mug, mix the red wine vinegar, sugar, soy, water and cornflour together. Add to the pan and stir well; the sauce should thicken.

5 Serve the fish on top of the mash and pour the sauce over.

PRAWN JAMBALAYA

GLUTEN-FREE: use GF chorizo and stock cubes.

1 ½ mugs (375g) **basmati rice**

1 tablespoon **olive oil**

1 **onion**, chopped

1 clove **garlic**, chopped

½ **green pepper**, chopped

100g **diced chorizo**

1 teaspoon **chilli powder**

1 teaspoon **ground turmeric**

6 medium **tomatoes**, chopped

½ mug (150ml) **water**

1 **chicken stock cube**

350g **cooked prawns**

1 tablespoon freshly chopped **coriander**

1 Cook the rice and leave in the pan, with the lid on, until needed.

2 Heat the oil in a wok or large frying pan. Add the onion, garlic and pepper and cook until they begin to soften. Add the chorizo and fry until it begins to brown.

3 Add the chilli powder, turmeric, tomatoes, water and stock cube and bring to the boil. Simmer for 2 minutes.

4 Add the prawns and coriander and cook for 1 minute.

5 Stir in the cooked rice and serve.

🐾 COOK FOOLPROOF RICE: FOR 4 PEOPLE, PUT 3 MUGS BOILING WATER IN A PAN, ADD 1 1/2 MUGS BASMATI RICE. BRING TO THE BOIL. SIMMER GENTLY WITH A LID ON THE PAN FOR 10 MINUTES. THE WATER SHOULD BE ABSORBED AND THE RICE FLUFFY.

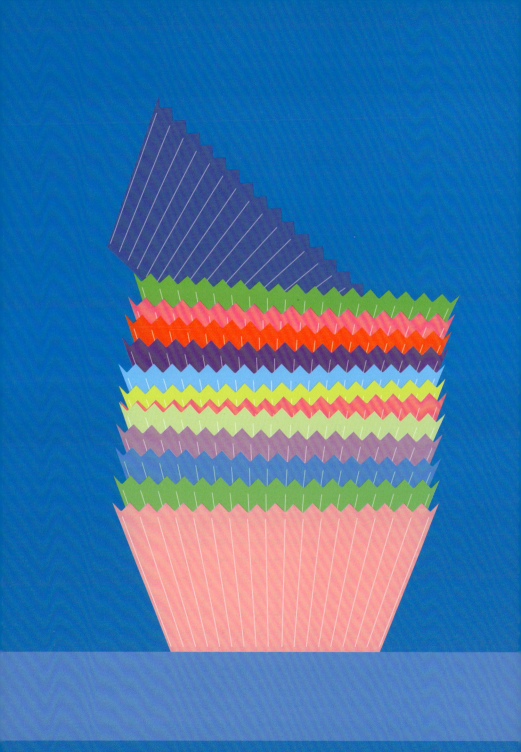

BAKING & DESSERTS

Love cakes and cookies, but don't want complicated and lengthy prep? I have included some that only take 25 minutes from start to finish. When Ben is craving chocolate, he sometimes challenges me to see how quickly I can make him some chocolate cookies. My fastest, so far, has been 22 minutes, but that is with a bit of practice! The 'Brioche Pudding' takes only 5-10 minutes to prepare and is delicious.

ORANGE & GINGER COOKIES WITH PECANS

You can actually leave this dough for a couple of days in the fridge and cook fresh cookies whenever you want them.

175g softened **butter**, measure using packet

3/4 mug (175g) **granulated sugar**

1 **egg**

zest of an **orange**

1 tablespoon juice from **orange**

2 mugs (360g) **self-raising flour**

50g **pecan nuts**, chopped

4 pieces **crystallised ginger,** chopped

1 Beat the butter and sugar together in a mixing bowl until it is light and fluffy.

2 Add the egg, orange rind and orange juice and beat until smooth.

3 Add the flour, pecans and ginger and mix to a dough.

4 Turn out onto a floured surface and divide into 2. Roll each half into a 'sausage' about 4cm in diameter. Wrap in cling film and leave in the fridge for 45 minutes.

5 Preheat the oven to 180°C fan/200°C/gas 6. Grease or line a baking tray.

6 The cookie dough will be quite firm by now. Cut with a sharp knife into 1cm thick cookies and place on the baking tray 4cm apart. Bake in the oven for 10 minutes. The cookies will be slightly browned around the edges.

SMARTIE OAT COOKIES

125g softened **butter**, measure using packet

1 mug (200g) **soft brown sugar**

1 teaspoon **vanilla extract**

1 **egg**

1 mug (170g) **self-raising flour**

150g pack **Smarties**

1/2 mug (100g) **oats**

1 tablespoon **cocoa**

Smarties to decorate

1 Preheat the oven to 180°C fan/200°C/gas 6. Grease 2 baking trays.

2 Beat the butter and sugar together. Add the vanilla extract and egg and beat well.

3 Add the flour, Smarties, oats and cocoa. Mix to a stiff dough.

4 Roll into a 30cm 'sausage' and cut into about 24 cookies. Place on the baking trays. Leave space between them, as they spread out. Press a few Smarties in each to decorate.

5 Place in the oven for 12 minutes. The cookies should be crisp on the outside and a little chewy on the inside.

SCAN ME

🌐 **SEE MORE CAKES AND COOKIE RECIPES ONLINE: WWW.NOSHBOOKS.COM/COOKIE**

ALMOND & WHITE CHOCOLATE CHIP COOKIES

125g softened **butter**, measure using packet

3/4 mug (200g) **soft brown sugar**

1 **egg**

1 teaspoon **almond extract**

1 1/4 mugs (225g) **self-raising flour**

100g packet **white chocolate chips**

1/2 mug (50g) **desiccated coconut**

1/2 mug (60g) **toasted flaked almonds**

1 Preheat the oven to 180°C fan/200°C/gas 6. Grease 2 baking trays.

2 Beat the butter and sugar together until pale in colour.

3 Add the egg and almond extract and beat until smooth.

4 Add the flour and chocolate chips. Gently mix together to form a soft dough.

5 Divide the mixture into approximately 30 small balls.

6 Put the coconut and almonds on a plate and mix together. Press the dough balls into the coconut and almonds.

7 Place the balls on the baking trays, about 5cm apart, as the dough will spread in the oven.

8 Place in the oven for 14 minutes until the cookies are pale brown. Leave to cool on the trays. The cookies should be crunchy on the outside and a bit chewy on the inside.

ALMOND & POPPY SEED COOKIES

The unusual addition of cream cheese to these cookies ensures that they stay gooey and chewy in the centre.

50g softened **butter**, measure using packet

75g **Philadelphia cream cheese**

1 ¼ mugs (225g) **granulated sugar**

1 **egg**

1 teaspoon **vanilla extract**

1 teaspoon **almond extract**

1 mug (210g) **self-raising flour**

1 tablespoon **poppy seeds**

½ mug (50g) **toasted flaked almonds**

1 Preheat the oven to 180°C fan/200°C/gas 6. Grease 2 baking trays.

2 Beat together the butter, cream cheese and sugar until light and fluffy.

3 Add the egg, vanilla and almond extract and beat well.

4 Add the flour and poppy seeds and mix to a dough.

5 Divide into approximately 30 pieces and roll into balls. Roll them in the flaked almonds. Place on the baking trays and squash each one down a little.

6 Bake in the oven for 12 minutes; the cookies should be slightly browned. They will be slightly chewy in the middle and crisp on the outside.

CHOCOLATE ORANGE FUDGE FINGERS

75g **dark chocolate**, broken up

2 tablespoons **cocoa**

1 mug (200g) **soft brown sugar**

1/3 mug (100ml) **hot water**

175g softened **butter**, measure using packet

2 **eggs**

zest of an **orange**

1/2 mug (110g) **self-raising flour**

1/2 teaspoon **baking powder**

125ml **soured cream**

100g **chocolate**

1 Preheat the oven to 160°C fan/180°C/gas 4. Grease and line a baking tray.

2 Put the chocolate, cocoa and sugar in a food processor and blitz until it resembles crumbs. Add the hot water and blitz for 1 minute. If you do not have a food processor, just grate the chocolate and mix with the sugar, then add the hot water.

3 Add the butter and blitz for 30 seconds. Add the eggs and orange rind and blitz again. Add the flour, baking powder and soured cream and pulse a couple of times.

4 Pour onto the baking tray and put in the oven for 50 minutes. The top should have formed a crust, but the centre will still be a little soggy. Leave to cool.

5 Melt the chocolate in a bowl over simmering water. Drizzle over the cake and allow to set. Cut into whatever shapes you like.

APRICOT GOODY BARS
WITH PISTACHIOS & PUMPKIN SEEDS

Good alternative to the expensive 'goody bars' available in the supermarkets. Wrap in greaseproof paper if you want to add them to lunch boxes.

GLUTEN-FREE: use GF oats.

140g **butter**, measure using packet

1 mug (200g) **soft brown sugar**

2 tablespoons **runny honey**

2 mugs (200g) **rolled oats**

1/2 mug (75g) **pistachio nuts**

2/3 mug (100g) **ready-to-eat-dried apricots**, chopped

2/3 mug (150g) **raisins**

1/3 mug (50g) **pumpkin seeds**

1 Preheat the oven to 160°C fan/180°C/gas 4. Grease and line a 20x30cm traybake tin.

2 Put the butter, sugar and honey in a small pan and heat gently until the butter has melted and the sugar dissolved.

3 In a large bowl, mix the oats, pistachios, apricots, raisins and pumpkin seeds together.

4 Add the contents of the pan and mix together well.

5 Tip into the tin and press down evenly.

6 Place in the oven for 30–35 minutes; the top should be lightly browned.

7 Leave to cool and then cut into small squares.

CHOCOLATE FUDGE CAKE

2 **eggs**
½ mug (150ml) **sunflower oil**
½ mug (150ml) **milk**
397g tin **Carnation Caramel**
1 mug (175g) **self-raising flour**
2 ½ tablespoons **cocoa**
1 teaspoon **bicarb soda**
⅔ mug (150g) **caster sugar**
125g **dark chocolate**

1 Preheat the oven to 160°C fan/180°C/gas 4. Line 2 x 18cm round cake tins.

2 Whisk together the eggs, oil, milk, and 3 tablespoons of Carnation Caramel until smooth.

3 Mix the flour, cocoa, bicarb and sugar in a large bowl. Add the wet ingredients and mix together gently until smooth.

4 Pour into the 2 tins. It will look as though there is not enough mixture in the tins, but it will rise in the oven. Bake in the oven for 25 minutes.

5 Melt the chocolate in a bowl over a pan of simmering water. Add the rest of the Carnation Caramel and whisk until smooth. Once the cakes have cooled, put ⅓ of the topping in the middle of the cake and the other ⅔ on the top and side.

SCAN ME

🌐 **MINT AND CHOCOLATE ARE A GREAT COMBO. AGREE? HAVE A LOOK HERE: WWW.NOSHBOOKS.COM/MINT-SLICES**

INSTANT YOGURT ICE CREAM

You don't necessarily need a food processor or hand-held blender for this recipe. Just squish the raspberries with a spoon and add to the yogurt. You could eat this straight away, but putting it in the freezer firms it up so you can scoop it. Don't leave in the freezer for longer than 90 minutes, as the ice cream becomes quite hard.

500g **frozen raspberries**

2 mugs (600ml) **Greek yogurt**

2 tablespoons **runny honey**

CHOCOLATE SAUCE

25g **butter**, measure using packet

100g **milk chocolate**

1/2 mug (150ml) **double cream**

1 Put the raspberries, yogurt and honey in a food processor and blitz until the raspberries are completely broken up. Transfer into a dish, or plastic tub, and put in the freezer for 90 minutes.

2 Make the chocolate sauce. Put the ingredients in a small saucepan and gently heat. Allow to bubble for 30 seconds. Set to one side until needed.

3 Serve together.

STRAWBERRY & ALMOND PAVLOVAS

1 tablespoon **soft brown sugar**

3 **egg whites**

3/4 mug (170g) **caster sugar**

1/4 mug (35g) **toasted flaked almonds**

juice of an **orange**

1/4 x 454g jar **blackcurrant jelly jam**

500g **strawberries**

300ml **double cream**

1 Preheat the oven to 150°C fan/170°C/gas 3. Line 2 baking trays with greaseproof paper.

2 Line another baking tray with greaseproof paper and sprinkle the brown sugar over it. Place under the grill until the sugar melts and begins to bubble. You need to watch the sugar as it will quickly burn. Leave to cool and then crush, with a spoon, or blitz in a processor.

3 Whisk the egg whites in a clean bowl until stiff. Gradually add the caster sugar and beat well until the sugar is dissolved; this should make quite a stiff mixture. Fold in the caramelised sugar and almonds.

4 Spoon tablespoons of the mixture onto the baking sheets; it should make about 8. Place in the oven for 40 minutes. Turn off the oven and leave the meringues in there for another 1050 minutes.

5 Put the orange juice and jam in a small pan and gently heat until the jam has dissolved. Chop up the strawberries and add to the pan. Leave to cool.

6 Beat the cream to soft peaks.

7 Serve the meringues with a dollop of cream and the strawberry mixture.

🌐 SEE ANOTHER PAVLOVA RECIPE HERE:
WWW.NOSHBOOKS.COM/ALMOND-AND-PEAR-PAVLOVA

SCAN ME

BRIOCHE PUDDING

A truly yummy alternative to plain old bread and butter pudding. This could barely be simpler to make. Slice the bread, pour everything over the top and wack in the oven.

butter to grease the dish
400g **brioche loaf**
250g **frozen raspberries**
4 **eggs**
300ml **single cream**
2 tablespoons **caster sugar**
grated zest of a **lemon**
1 teaspoon **vanilla extract**

1 Preheat the oven to 160°C fan/180°C/gas 5. Grease a casserole dish with butter.

2 Cut the brioche into 1cm slices and arrange them in the dish. Add the raspberries and tuck them into the bread (see photo).

3 Beat the eggs in a bowl and add the cream, sugar, lemon rind and vanilla. Pour over the brioche as evenly as possible. Leave to stand for 5 minutes, to allow the brioche to absorb the liquid.

4 Place in the oven for 20-25 minutes. The brioche should be lightly browned and the egg mixture set.

STRAWBERRY MUFFIN 'MILLEFEUILLE'

MUFFINS

2 2/3 mugs (525g) **self-raising flour** minus 2 tablespoons

2 tablespoons **cocoa**

1 mug (175g) **granulated sugar**

100g **white choc chips**

100g **milk choc chips**

2 **eggs**, beaten

1 1/2 mugs (450ml) **milk**

3/4 mug (225ml) **vegetable oil**

15 large **muffin cases**

CHOCOLATE SAUCE

100g **milk chocolate**

25g **butter**, measure using packet

300ml **double cream**

2 tablespoons **soft brown sugar**

300ml **double cream**

500g **strawberries**

1 Preheat the oven to 180°C fan/200°C/gas 6. Prepare 15 large muffin cases in muffin tins.

2 To make the muffins, put all the dry ingredients in a large bowl. Mix together the wet ingredients in a large jug. Pour into the bowl and mix together. Put 2 dessertspoons of the mixture in each cake case. Place in the oven for 25 minutes, or until the cakes bounce back a little when they are lightly pressed. Leave to cool.

3 To make the chocolate sauce, place all the sauce ingredients in a small saucepan and gently bring to the boil. Simmer for 30 seconds and then leave to cool a little.

4 Beat the cream until it just begins to thicken, but not really stiff.

5 Cut the strawberries into small pieces. Cut the muffin into 3 slices.

6 Assemble everything - see photo - words escape me as to how I explain this one!

MARS BAR CHOCOLATE SAUCE WITH ICE CREAM & BLUEBERRIES

This sauce is naughty, but nice. As long as we don't eat it everyday, just for a treat, I think we will survive!

SAUCE

3 **Mars bars**, chopped
300ml **double cream**
100g **marshmallows**

tub of **ice cream**
150g **blueberries**
1 extra **Mars bar** to decorate!

1 Put the sauce ingredients in a saucepan and heat gently until everything melts.

2 Serve with the ice cream and blueberries.

BAILEYS TIRAMISU

CHOCOLATE SAUCE

25g **butter**, measure using packet

100g **milk chocolate**

¼ mug (50g) **soft brown sugar**

½ mug (150ml) **double cream**

1 tablespoon **cocoa**

250g **mascarpone**

300ml **double cream**

285g **Madeira cake**

2 teaspoons **instant coffee** in 1 tablespoon **hot water**

½ mug (150ml) **Baileys**

3 tablespoons **toasted flaked almonds**

1 tablespoon **cocoa**

1 To make the chocolate sauce, melt the butter and chocolate in a small saucepan, add the sugar, cream and cocoa. Heat gently until everything is combined and the sugar dissolved. Set to one side to cool slightly.

2 Gently mix together the mascarpone and the mug of double cream. Set to one side.

3 Cut the Madeira cake into thin strips and line the bottom of a trifle bowl. Mix the water and instant coffee together and then add to the Baileys. Pour evenly over the cake.

4 Pour the chocolate sauce over the cake.

5 Gently spoon the mascarpone mix over and gently smooth over.

6 Sprinkle the almonds on top and then sieve the cocoa over.

7 Leave in the fridge for about 1 hour. It is best eaten within 2 hours, but is also still yummy the next day.

GET OUT ALL THE INGREDIENTS BEFORE YOU START; IT MAKES COOKING A LOT CALMER.

index